The Wicked

Lord Lyttelton

The *Wicked*
Lord Lyttelton

Thomas Frost

NONSUCH

First published 1876
Copyright © in this edition 2006
Nonsuch Publishing Ltd

Nonsuch Publishing Limited
The Mill, Brimscombe Port, Stroud, Gloucestershire, GL5 2QG
www.nonsuch-publishing.com

Nonsuch Publishing Ltd is an imprint of the Tempus Publishing Group

British Library Cataloguing in Publication Data.
A catalogue record for this book is available from the British Library.

ISBN 1-84588-078-1

Typesetting and origination by Nonsuch Publishing Limited
Printed in Great Britain by Oaklands Book Services Limited

CONTENTS

INTRODUCTION TO THE MODERN EDITION

THOMAS, SECOND BARON Lyttelton (1744–1779), known as 'the wicked Lord Lyttelton' (in contrast to his father, George, the first Baron, who was 'the good Lord Lyttelton'), is perhaps a victim of the censorious gossip of fashionable mid-eighteenth-century 'society.' Though chiefly remembered for being 'wicked,' his offences were probably no worse than those of any other young man of the period: he gambled, ran up debts, seduced women and fought duels, but this was scarcely unusual at the time. He was certainly not a pillar of moral rectitude, but neither was he totally dissipated, at least not in the latter part of his comparatively short life. There is perhaps some truth in his own belief that, had he found consistent political employment, he would have been less tempted to vice.

Lyttelton sat in the House of Commons from 1768–1769, where he made a good impression as an orator, but lost his seat because of allegations of electoral fraud. Early in 1774 his father died and he inherited the peerage and his seat in the House of Lords. 1774 was the year that events in Britain's North American colonies began to move inexorably towards independence, with Parliament passing the so-called Coercive or Punitive Acts in response to growing unrest there. It was also the year that the first Continental Congress met, which drafted the Articles of Association, an agreement by the colonies to boycott trade with Britain. In 1775 the American War of Independence began and

Lyttelton, despite being an independent with Whig tendencies, supported the Tory administration. In return for his support, he was appointed to the sinecure of Chief Justice in Eyre north of the River Trent and made a Privy Councillor.

Following the Battles of Lexington and Concord, which the colonists won, and the Battle of Bunker Hill, which the British won, but at great cost, the Continental Congress sent the Olive Branch Petition to King George III proposing reconciliation, but it was rejected out of hand. 1776 saw the signing of the Declaration of Independence; the Articles of Confederation, the first governing document of the United States, were adopted by the second Continental Congress in 1777. France officially recognised the new republic and declared war on Britain in 1778. The possibility of Spain joining France in opposing Britain and the failure of a British fleet to defeat the French in the first Battle of Ushant induced Lord Lyttelton to criticise the way in which the government was conducting the war and advocate the abandonment of party divisions in the interests of the country. This, however, did not happen, and the War was to continue for another four years after his death.

Lyttelton's attitude to Ireland was somewhat less imperialistic than his attitude towards North America. Unusually, he took the trouble to visit the country before voicing his opinion in Parliament. He was in favour of allowing the Irish free trade and the same constitutional freedoms as England. When France entered the War of American Independence against Britain, Ireland was threatened with invasion. The Irish asked for troops, but were told to defend themselves as all available soldiers were in North America. Therefore the Irish formed associations to defend themselves, which the British government then condemned as unconstitutional. Lyttelton pointed out the contradictory nature of this stance and spoke in favour of redressing some of Ireland's grievances.

Although Lord Lyttelton's political career was short, it is apparent that he was an able politican. Had he lived longer, he would doubtless have ascended to high office and his 'wickedness,' such as it was, would probably have been forgotten.

PREFACE

THOMAS, LORD LYTTELTON, the second Baron, commonly mentioned as "the wicked Lord Lyttelton," was, in many respects, one of the most remarkable characters of the century in which he lived. Accomplished, witty, clever, a brilliant orator, a good debater, an amusing letter-writer, the life and delight of every circle he joined, he shone like a meteor in society and politics for a few years, and invested even his last moments with an amount of interest which has seldom, if ever, been excelled. Yet there are few men who have ever occupied public attention in the same degree while living about whom so little is generally known. The majority, even of the educated, have no other impression concerning him, than that he was a gambler and a libertine, who outraged every moral law, and created a sensation in the world when about to leave it, by prophesying the hour of his death, on the authority of a supposed supernatural visitation.

The causes of the prevalence of this view of the position which Thomas Lyttelton held in the society and politics of his time are easily to be found by those who will take the trouble to seek them. During the greater part of his life, he was estranged from his family, every member of which avoided even the mention of his name. Numerous as are the published letters of his father, he is mentioned in them only once or twice after attaining his majority, and then only in the slightest manner. The biographers of his father scarcely mention him. The memoir-writers of the latter part of the eighteenth century record only the gossip of club and coterie concerning his death. Horace Walpole, who mentions him more frequently than any other diarist or letter-writer of the period, never fails to depreciate him in every possible way, and to strive to convey the impression that he was as contemptible as he was reported to be profligate.

This persistent endeavour to ignore the man altogether, and to depreciate his character and abilities when that course became impossible, cannot be accounted for by his evil repute as a gambler and a rake. There were worse men in both Houses of Parliament than Thomas Lyttelton. There were some who, with the same faults and without greater abilities, have become celebrated; there were more who did not possess half his talent and eloquence, and yet were better remembered. How is it, then, that he has been known for nearly a century as "the wicked Lord Lyttelton," and nothing more?

It seems to me that the motive for the general desire to ignore or depreciate Thomas Lyttelton may be found in the independence of party of which he was almost an unique example in his day, and which must have rendered him to his contemporaries a political anomaly. Though he held office under a Tory minister, his speeches, equally with his letters, evince a regard for civil and religious freedom greater than was felt by some, even of those who sat on the benches of the Opposition. There was no one among the Whigs who spoke more strongly against the North Ministry than he did whenever he believed them to be in the wrong. On one occasion he declared himself as genuine a Whig as the Earl of Chatham. "I love Whig principles," he said, "as much as I despise those of anarchy and republicanism. But if the bare name of Whig is all that is meant, I disclaim it." As that political phenomenon, an independent member of a Ministry— the position claimed to be held by Sir Robert Peel in 1854, to the disgust of the partisans of the then existing Government, and the amusement of its opponents—he could not fail to be misunderstood, suspected, reviled, even if he had been the most virtuous man in the kingdom.

He was suspected, moreover, of holding the sceptical views of revealed religion which were then beginning to prevail among the educated classes of continental Europe. There is not only no proof that he held such views, but the strongest reasons for believing that, inconsistent with the requirements of a Christian life as his conduct often was, he entertained the most profound respect for the Gospel. He certainly always professed such a respect, and there seems no reason to doubt that he felt it. No one ever accused him of being hypocritical or dishonest, but he read the works of deistical authors, and that was sufficient for his condemnation. The hands of his pious father and right reverend uncle were held up in horror, and, as the semblance of piety was fashionable in those days, than which none have been marked more strongly with corruption and immorality, society shrank from him as a matter of decorum, if not of loyalty.

Thomas Lyttelton was not a virtuous man. Virtuous men were scarce in those days, and it cannot be claimed for the subject of this biography that he was one of the comparatively few exceptions to the general rule. But it may fairly be doubted whether his character has not been unfairly blackened. Some of the scandals associated with his name, which have been repeated by successive writers, without inquiry, have proved, on investigation, to have no other foundation to rest upon than the idlest rumour. Others have been so variously related by different narrators as to sufficiently testify, by their variations, to their mythical character. It was the common belief of that generation that a man or woman who was sceptical on the subject of revealed religion must necessarily be abandoned to every kind of wickedness, and such scepticism being unfairly attributed to Thomas Lyttelton, he became the dog with an ill name, whom it was an evidence of piety and respectability to abuse.

In gathering materials for this biography it was impossible to disregard the collection of letters edited by William Combe, author of the amusing poetical record of the "Travels and Adventures of Dr. Syntax." That industrious *littérateur* was a schoolfellow of Thomas Lyttelton, at Eton. Having dissipated a good fortune by gambling, he adopted literature as a profession, and worked indefatigably for many years at compiling, editing, translating, and contributing letters and articles upon almost every topic to newspapers and magazines. Of his comparatively few original works, "Dr. Syntax" is the only one which has survived him. He seems to have been always at the beck of the booksellers—equally ready to write a pamphlet, which should bear on its title-page the name of a peer or M.P., to supply a sermon for a preacher with more money than brains, or to produce a biography for publication on the day after the decease of its subject.

Shortly after the death of Thomas Lyttelton a volume of letters appeared, with the title—"Letters of the late Lord Lyttelton." The executors of the deceased nobleman at once pronounced them to be forgeries, but no grounds were assigned by them for that statement, which does not appear to have received much credit, since the sale of the book was sufficient to induce the publishers to issue a second volume two years afterwards. How, indeed, could his executors, only one of whom had been on intimate terms with him, be in a position to be cognisant of every letter he had ever written? The Lyttelton family may have had good reasons for desiring the suppression of the correspondence; but they were the last persons likely to know much about the matter of which they pretended to judge. They condemned as spurious, with equal confidence, many of the poems published in 1780, as the works of the deceased nobleman, though the volume was edited by his friend Roberts, who was one of his executors, and to whom he bequeathed all his MSS. at his death.

The letters were alleged by the Lyttelton family to have been concocted, as a literary speculation, by William Combe. It will be shown, however, that there are matters of family interest mentioned in them which Combe could not have known. There is no doubt that Combe edited both volumes, and it has been conjectured,[1] without any show of reason, that he may have made alterations and additions: the hypothesis is purely gratuitous. Nichol[2] treated the letters as genuine; and the author of the article in the *Quarterly*, just alluded to, was of the same opinion.

The late John Camden Hotten[3] claimed them, however, as an undoubted production of Combe's, on the authority of an article by Mr. Robert Cole,[4] in which a list of Combe's works appeared, the original of which was stated to be in his own handwriting, and in the possession of the writer of the article. It appears that Ackermann, the publisher, for whom Combe sometimes did literary work, had asked the veteran for a complete list of his productions; and the letter containing the request (dated eleven days before Combe's death), with the list and a duplicate, were found at the latter's lodging in Lambeth. In this list there certainly appears this entry: "Lord Lyttelton's Letters. 2 vols. duod." This, in the opinion of John Camden Hotten, was conclusive evidence that the letters were not the genuine correspondence of Thomas Lyttelton, but the spurious productions of the clever William Combe.

Unfortunately for this characteristically cool and reckless assumption, the list includes also Anderson's "History of Commerce," Foote's "Life of Murphy," Anderson's "History of the Embassy to China," Anderson's "History of the Campaign in Egypt," Sir Alexander Mackenzie's "Journey across North America," and the same traveller's "Voyage to South America,"— which he merely revised for republication, or gave literary assistance in! John Camden Hotten has gone where he cannot write letters to explain his reasons for believing that Combe wrote the letters published as Lord Lyttelton's, though he certainly did not write the other works just mentioned, the evidence in both cases being the same: but the readers of the following biography will have no difficulty in forming a sound judgment upon the question.

Little more value can be attached to the documentary evidence on the subject with which I have been favoured, for the purpose of this work, by the present Lord Lyttelton than to the list of Combe's "works" given to the world by Mr. Robert Cole. The evidence to which I allude is neither more nor less than the confession of William Combe himself that he was the author of the letters attributed to Thomas Lord Lyttelton; and it was made

very circumstantially to Major Cockburn, and communicated by
that gentleman to Mr. J. Lyttelton, of Wimbledon Park, Surrey,
in the following letter:—

"Woolwich, *May* 19*th*, 1818.
"DEAR SIR,—When I had the pleasure of meeting you at
the theatre, you expressed a wish to know the particulars of a
conversation that took place between Mr. Combe and myself,
relating to Lord Lyttelton. I have seen Mr. C. on this subject, and
now send you what he said, word for word.

"'At the German Spa, about the year 1782, a Mrs. H., a sort
of literary lady, and whom I had known for some years, had
brought from England Lord L.'s poems, then lately published, as
I understood by Miles Peter Andrews, a gunpowder gentleman,
whom that nobleman brought into Parliament for Bewdley.
Mrs. H., who was a contemporary with me in the great and
fashionable world, when I moved in that sphere, and knew some
little circumstances that took place between Lord (when Mr.) L.
and myself, which made no common noise at the period, as an
inducement for me to breakfast with her, said she would add a
plate of *jeux d'esprit* that must very much interest me. I went, and
beheld the poems, in the form of a quarto pamphlet. They were
all of them familiar acquaintances of mine that used to occupy
a portfolio in the *sanctum sanctorum*—God forgive me!—in
Curzon Street, where the old lord lived above, and his son and
heir lived below.

"'My recollection at this moment would enable me to give a
very curious comparative history of those two apartments, and
of the two distinct personages who occupied them; for I was
equally well received by both, and I remember, to my no small
satisfaction, that, difficult as the task might be, I did not play
the hypocrite with either. Oh, what two conversations I could
repeat, on two successive mornings, between the noble father,
the right reverend uncle of Carlisle, the Reverend Dr. De Salis,
and myself; and, on the following day, between the noble son—a
sneaking, sycophantic, but learned Scotchman,—Dr. Baylis, a

Worcestershire physician transplanted to London—a gentleman of genius, known by the name of Mad Henley—and the self-same expletive, which L. used to honour with three titles, and at this distance of time they may be mentioned without vanity—the immovable, the fascinating, and polished C. And on which three denominations, as you have caused me to touch the spring of a secret drawer in the cabinet of my memory, which has not been examined for so many years, I now find sufficient materials to form a volume.

"'This episode you will excuse, but it is connected most intimately in my mind with the poems which I left upon Mrs. H.'s breakfast-table at Spa, whither I must beg leave to reconduct you. I read them aloud, and to my surprise found two of my own trifles among them. Compliments passed, and it was wished that some more from the same mind had been added. In short, the conversation terminated in my engaging to do something *à la* Lyttelton that might be received as his. I accordingly turned my thoughts to "Dialogues of the Dead." He, I knew, had written some to ridicule those of his father⁵ and Mrs. Montagu. I remember three of them, and have them somewhere among my immense cargo of papers, the waste of between fifty and sixty years. They were, if I recollect right, replete with wit, spirit, and blasphemy, and patriotism. The parties were King David of Israel and Cæsar Borgia, the Saviour of the world and Socrates, Epaminondas and General Wolfe.

"'However, I changed my plan, for very evident reasons, and began a series of letters, one or more of which were thought to form an amusing article at Mrs. H.'s breakfast till the materials of the first volume were completed. She requested the manuscripts, and I presented them to her. She took them to England, where they became an object of curiosity in her circle. On her persuasion, I consented to their publication. The public received them with great avidity, when the family thought proper to advertise them in the public papers as an imposition, which they certainly were; but, as they were not discreditable to his character; they were rather to blame to consider the writer of them, whom they did not know, in the view in which they thought proper to represent, or rather misrepresent him. I accordingly, by a counter advertisement, dated Edinburgh, but written at Brussels, insisted upon their originality, and promised another volume, which I wrote in the capital of Brabant. And here the work closed. Though the bookseller offered me 200 guineas, which he afterwards advanced to 300, for another volume, and offered 500 if I would make it two, and I had materials for three or four, with many curious histories, which I have not yet forgotten; but I had a respect for the family, which was fruitful in virtues, and whose weaknesses— for there was a little sprinkle of them—were such as are generally associated with worthy qualities.

"'It is curious enough that the old Lady Lyttelton, the widow of the first lord—a fine, obstinate, clever woman—used to abuse the family to the last hour of her life, and to that period I knew her, for denying the authenticity of these letters; and this she has done to me fifty times. The last summer she passed at her cottage at Ripley, in Surrey, at her particular request, I read the letters through to her. Her observations, as you may suppose, which were very frequent, very angry, very severe, and not without that wit which she eminently possessed, were very amusing to me; and the Spanish Minister, Del Campo, who passed a couple of days there during this lecture, and who knew the author, made the sofa upon which he lay shake from his occasional bursts of laughter, and did not escape frequent sallies of her lively reproach for so treating the beautiful compositions, as she was pleased to call them, of her son, as she was also pleased to call him, as she declared that the concentrated genius of Spain, and all the doctors of Salamanca, and the Archbishop of Toledo at their head, could not produce any thing like them.'

"I have finished this curious account, and have only one remark to make. Mr. C. wished to know, previous to his relating it, whether I wanted it for publication. I told him certainly not; I only wished to mention it to a friend. To this he had no objection.—I remain, dear sir, your obedient servant,

"J. COCKBURN."

I have given this story of Combe's in all its minuteness of detail as the best means of enabling my readers to form a sound judgment of it, and of the man by whom it was told. The inordinate vanity and coxcombry of his character are revealed in every sentence, and it is impossible to avoid the conclusion that he told the story (first taking the precaution to ascertain that it was not to receive publicity,) because his vanity was tickled in a greater degree by being thought the author of the letters than by being regarded as merely their editor. If he had been the forger and liar he confesses himself to have been, would he have revelled, as he evidently did, in all the details of the story, in the presence of an honourable man? Such an exhibition can be reconciled with the theory that the letters were spurious only by the supposition that Combe had fallen so low at this time as to be utterly insensible to shame. But on this hypothesis what credit is due to his confession?

It is a remarkable circumstance, not to be overlooked in forming a judgment on this question, though it seems to have escaped the notice of everyone who has maintained the spuriousness of the letters, that it might have been solved as soon as it was raised by the persons to whom the letters were addressed. The names of some of them are discoverable even now, and at the time of their publication the friends of Thomas Lord Lyttelton could have had no difficulty in deciding the point by declaring their knowledge, or otherwise, of the letters. They did not do so, however, and the acceptance of the letters was all but universal. In after years, even the Lyttelton family did not seek to disturb the verdict by publishing the confession of Combe, which is now given to the world for the first time.

All the circumstances considered, I incline to the view that the letters were the genuine epistles of Thomas Lord Lyttelton, and I am strengthened in my belief by the strong similarity of their tone and style to those of the autograph letters of that nobleman with which I have been favoured by the present Lord Lyttelton, and which are scattered through the following pages. Seventy years having elapsed since the last edition of the letters edited by Combe was published, it is now a scarce book, and the copy in my possession is the only one which has ever come under my notice, with the exception of the copy in the library of the British Museum. I have drawn upon it, therefore, for many illustrations of Thomas Lyttelton's life and character, which I believe my readers will not be sorry to have. I have not been able, in every instance, to ascertain the precise date, or the person to whom the letter was addressed. In every instance in which I have supplied a name left blank by Combe, I have enclosed it between brackets.

T. FROST.

LONG DITTON, *January*, 1876.

1. *Quarterly Review*, December, 1851: art. "Junius."
2. "Literary Anecdotes of the Eighteenth Century."
3. Memoir of Combe, prefixed to Hotten's edition of "Dr. Syntax," 1868.
4. *Gentleman's Magazine*, May, 1852.
5. This accusation of Combe's is strenuously repelled in one of the letters which he wished Major Cockburn to believe were written by himself.

I

EDUCATION
AND DEVELOPMENT

THOMAS LYTTELTON, THE Second Baron of that name, was born on the 30th of January, 1744. His father was the son of Sir Thomas Lyttelton, of Hagley, in Worcestershire; and his mother, whom Sir George Lyttelton married in 1741, was Lucy Fortescue, a Devonshire lady, whose untimely death, five years after marriage, deprived the hope of the family of maternal care during the years when he most needed it, and afforded her husband a theme for the poetical effusion by which he is best known to the present generation of readers.

Young Lyttelton gave promise, at a very early age, of the intellectual ability displayed by so many of his family, and was in due time sent to Eton, where his conduct seems to have been as free from blame as his progress in his studies was remarkable. His father wrote in 1758, when Thomas was fourteen years of age, of "the promise afforded by his opening talents;" and in the following year, when the lad accompanied his father in a tour through Scotland, as far as Inverary, Lord Lyttelton—he had been raised to the peerage during the Pelham Administration for his opposition to Sir Robert Walpole—wrote to his brother William: "Much the greatest pleasure I had in my tour was from the company of my son, and from the approbation (I might say admiration) which his figure, behaviour, and parts drew from all sorts of people wherever he went. Indeed, his mother[1] has given him her *don de plaire*, and he joins to an excellent understanding the best of hearts, and more discretion and judgment than ever I observed in any young man except you."

During this Scottish tour young Lyttelton produced some views of the beautiful scenery through which he passed, which, though it is probable that some allowance must be made for partiality on the part of his critics, must have been above the average excellence of amateur productions, to have evoked such praise as was awarded them by Mrs. Montagu, in a letter to his father. "Mr. Lyttelton," says the lady, "is a charming painter. His views of Scotland appear as the scenes of Salvator Rosa would do, were they copied by Claude, whose sweet and lovely imagination would throw fine colours over the darkest parts, and give grace to the rudest objects. I design at some time to visit Scotland, but I do not expect more pleasure from Nature's pencil than I have had from his pen. I can trust with equal confidence and delight to all you say of him. Pray God preserve you to guide him, and preserve him to make you happy."

It is not surprising to find, combined with the admiration of Nature which is essential to the landscape artist, a love of the grandest conceptions of the poet; but it must surprise those who regard Thomas Lyttelton as a mere scapegrace, remarkable only for his profligacy and the strange circumstances that attended his death, to learn that his favourite poet was Milton. "Of all the poets that have graced ancient times, or delighted the latter ages," he says, in a letter to a friend, "Milton is my favourite. I think him superior to every other, and the writer of all others the best calculated to elevate the mind, to form a nobleness of taste, and to teach a bold, commanding, energetic language. I read him with delight as soon as I could read at all; and I remember, in my father's words, I gave the first token of premature abilities in the perusal of the 'Paradise Lost.' I was quite a boy when, in reading that poem, I was so forcibly struck with a passage, that I laid down the book with some violence on the table, and took a hasty turn to the other end of the room. Upon explaining the cause of this emotion to my father, he clasped me in his arms, smothered me with embraces, and immediately wrote letters to all his family and friends, to inform them of the wonderful foreboding I had given of future genius. Your curiosity may naturally expect to be gratified with the passage in question; I quote it, therefore, for your reflection and amusement:

> He spoke; and, to confirm his words, out flew
> Millions of flaming swords, drawn from the thighs
> Of mighty Cherubim: the sudden blaze
> Far round illumin'd Hell!"

Too much reason is afforded by the letters of his father, of Mrs. Montagu, and others, for the belief that the praises which his budding talents called forth were too lavishly and indiscriminately awarded to be good for the mental and moral health of their recipient. In after-life he saw the mistake that had been made, and complained of it with the bitterness that pervades many of the letters of the period when he roused himself for a time from the influence of the Circean draughts of which he had so deeply drunk. "I have been," he said, "the victim of vanity, and the sacrifice of me was begun before I could form a judgment of the passion." The friend to whom this remark was made wishing for its explanation, he wrote a letter, which will be further quoted in another chapter, and from which only as much need be given here as relates to the defects of his early training.

"You will," he says, "I believe, agree with me that vanity is the foible of my family. Every individual has a share of it for himself, and for the rest. They are all equally vain of themselves and of one another. It is not, however, an unamiable vanity: it makes them happy, though it may sometimes render them ridiculous; and it never did an injury to anyone but to me. I have every reason to load it with execration, and to curse the hour when this Passion was concentrated to myself. Being the only boy, and hope of the family, and having such an hereditary and collateral right to genius, talents, and virtue (for this was the language held by certain persons at that time), my earliest prattle was the subject of continual admiration. As I increased in years, I was encouraged in boldness, which partial fancy called manly confidence; while sallies of impertinence, for which I should have been scourged, were fondly considered as marks of an astonishing prematurity of abilities. As it happened, Nature had not been a niggard to me. It is true she has given me talents, but accompanied them with dispositions which demanded no common repressure and restraint, instead of liberty and encouragement. But this vanity had blinded the eyes, not only of my relations, but also of their intimate connections; and, I suppose, such an hot-bed of flattery was never before used to spoil a mind, and to choke it with bad qualities, as was applied to mine. The late Lord Bath, Mrs. Montagu, and many others, have been guilty of administering fuel to the flame, and joined in the family incense to such an idol as myself. Thus was I nursed into a very early state of audacity; and being able, almost at all times, to get the laugh against a father, or an uncle, I was not backward in giving such impertinent specimens of my ability. This is the history of that impudence which has been my bane, gave to my excesses such peculiar accompaniments, and caused those who would not have hesitated to commit the offence loudly to condemn the mode of its commission in me."

One specimen of the praise that Lord Lyttelton lavished upon his son has been given. That he wrote of him to Mrs. Montagu in terms equally eulogistic may be gathered from a letter from that lady to his lordship, written in August, 1759, in which she says: "Your lordship's commendations of Mr. Lyttelton not only make me happy, but make me vain. He is every day going on to complete all I have wished and predicted on this subject." Earl Temple joined in the chorus of praise, as we learn from a letter addressed in after years to its object, in which he says: "I have in very early days acknowledged and done justice to your talents."[2] Dr. Barnard, the headmaster at Eton, often compared Thomas Lyttelton with Charles James Fox, to the advantage of the former; and though it must be remembered that young Lyttelton was five years the senior of the future Prime Minister of England, it is probable that Dr. Barnard was not unmindful of the difference of age, and had in his mind, when making the comparison long after both men had left Eton, the intellectual powers which they had respectively displayed at the same age. The master's estimate has been thought partial. But it is impossible to compare the oratorical efforts and few literary productions of both men without feeling that the intellectual superiority assigned to Lyttelton was a reality, and that he might, had he attained the same years as Fox, have achieved greater distinctions both in literature and in politics. At Eton, and at the same age, there was no reason to anticipate for Fox a degree of fame and distinction higher than might be won by Lyttelton.

But for the injudicious training that developed the foibles that should have been counteracted, and the undiscriminating flattery that was lavished upon him by all with whom he came in contact, the youth of Thomas Lyttelton would have been passed under favourable auspices. His father was honoured with the friendship of the Prince of Wales and the leading men of the day; he was a Privy Councillor, a Lord of the Treasury, and, later, Chancellor of the Exchequer. The future peer enjoyed the advantage of social intercourse with most of those who had achieved political or literary distinction, his father blending both characters, and being a patron of literary men, as well as himself a contributor to the literature of the period. It was Lord Lyttelton who obtained for Thomson his pension, and for Fielding his appointment as a magistrate; he was the first to encourage the poetical efforts of Mickle, who came to London when Thomas Lyttelton was twenty years of age, and he was a fellow-labourer with Horace Walpole, Soame Jenyns, the Earl of Chesterfield, and other remarkable men, in the columns of the *World*.

"Coventry dined yesterday at Claremont," says George James Williams—commonly called Gilly Williams—in a letter to George Selwyn, written in the summer of 1763, when Thomas Lyttelton was in his twentieth year. "The dinner consisted of Lord Spencer, the Rockinghams, little Villiers, Lord Lyttelton and his son, General Mostyn, and his lordship." Claremont was at that time the seat of the first Duke of Newcastle. This is the earliest mention of Thomas Lyttelton in the letters and memoirs of the period, subsequent to the date of the eulogies of Mrs. Montagu. He was the youngest of the party at Claremont, and may be excused if he felt a sense of rising importance in the world upon which he was preparing to enter, with all the *éclat* derivable from his father's social and political position and associations. As yet he viewed life through the "golden exhalations of the dawn," and everything was to his youthful vision beautiful and bright. A brilliant future was anticipated for him by all his friends; and the blight and chill of the future were as yet in the thoughts of none.

1.   Lord Lyttelton had married, in 1749, Elizabeth, daughter of
     Sir Robert Rich. The union was unfortunate, and resulted in
     separation.
2.   Correspondence of the Earl of Chatham, vol. iv., p. 222.

II

A EUROPEAN TOUR

About the time of the dinner at Claremont, a matrimonial project was planned by the Lyttelton family for its hope, the young heir of Hagley, and acceded to by him with a readiness which the beauty and amiability of the young lady of their choice sufficiently explains.

Miss Warburton, the only daughter of General Warburton, belonged to a good family, and possessed both great personal attractions and an excellent disposition, as well as a considerable fortune; and young Lyttelton, enraptured with her beauty, and viewing life through the rose-coloured glasses of youth, anticipated with eagerness the felicity which seemed to be in store for him. Letters are extant in which he speaks of Miss Warburton in the highest terms, and looks forward to their union with the most passionate devotion; and it is not improbable that, if this dream of his youth had been realised, he would have lived in the memory of posterity, not as "the wicked Lord Lyttelton," but as one of the greatest statesmen of the eighteenth century.

But, as he was at this time only nineteen years of age, and no marriage-settlement could be made until he had attained his majority, it was suggested by Sir Richard Lyttelton, one of his uncles, that he should pass the intervening time in travelling on the Continent. It does not seem the course best calculated to give steadiness to the character of a young man, who, from hints which he has given in letters written in after life, seems already to have shown symptoms of moral aberration, or to ensure the future happiness of the young persons whom it was thought desirable to unite in marriage, that they should not see each other during the period between betrothment and union, and that the interval should be passed by him in rambling with companions of his own age and dispositions from one foreign capital to another, and joining in the pleasures and dissipations of all. The admonition of Lord Burghley was thrown away upon Lord Lyttelton, and fashion and conventionality held their sway as potently as with inferior minds.

Thomas Lyttelton saw, later in life, the grievous mistake that was committed by his elders, and has placed on record his view of the matter in the letter quoted in the preceding chapter, and to which I now return. "When I drew towards manhood," he says, "it will be sufficient to say that I began to have some glimmering of the family weakness. However, I was still young, dependence was a considerable restraint, and I had not acquired that subsequent knowledge of the world which changed my notions of paternal authority. I was, therefore, without much difficulty brought to consent to the design of giving solidity to my character, and preserving me from public contagion by marriage. A rich and amiable young lady was chosen to the happy and honourable task of securing so much virtue as mine, to correct the natural exuberance of youthful inexperience, and to shape me into that perfection of character which was to verify the dreams of my visionary relations.

"I must own that the lady was both amiable and handsome, but cold as an anchorite; and, though formed to be the best wife in the world to a good husband, was by no means calculated to reclaim a bad one. But, to complete the sensible and well-digested plan, in which so many wise heads were concerned, it was determined for me to make the tour of Europe previous to my marriage, in order to perfectionate my matrimonial qualifications; and the lovely idea of the fair maid I left behind was presented to me as possessing a talismanic power to preserve me from seduction. But this was not all. For the better enabling me to make a proper and becoming appearance, or, in other words, to give me every means of gratification, the family purse was lavishly held forth; I was left almost without control in point of expense, and every method pursued to make me return the very reverse of what expectation had painted me."

The expenses of the Continental tour were borne by Sir Richard Lyttelton, a circumstance which explains the allusion to "the family purse." It may be remarked here that this circumstance was not likely to be known beyond the family circle, and its mention goes far to prove the genuineness of the letters which the Lytteltons strove to persuade the world were the spurious concoctions of William Combe, the author of "Dr. Syntax." How should this circumstance have been known to Combe? The fact itself does not rest solely on the authority of the letter that has been quoted; it is mentioned in a letter from Lord Lyttelton to his brother Richard.[1]

Thomas Lyttelton set out on his travels in the summer of 1763, and was either accompanied by John Damer, the eldest son of Lord Milton, and probably by that gentleman's brother George, or met them on the Continent. They had been at Eton together, and continued through life on terms of the closest intimacy. John Damer was the same age as Lyttelton, whom he resembled in temperament and aspirations.

It seems to have been contemplated at the outset that Lyttelton should have the advantage of paternal companionship and guidance during the greater part of the Continental tour; for his father wrote, towards the close of September, "He is just setting out from France to go to Italy, and I hope next summer to come to him at Florence, and make with him the tour of the Milanese, part of Germany, and all Switzerland by the end of October."[2] But this intention was not realised; and if the cause is to be found in the parental displeasure which Thomas Lyttelton soon evoked by the follies and dissipation in which he indulged during this tour, both he and his friends must have often regretted that an endeavour was not made to preserve him from the temptations with which a youth of rank and fortune could not fail to be beset while travelling through France and Italy with young men of his own age and of similar temperaments.

The first of the letters which the courtesy and kindness of the present Lord Lyttelton enables me to place before my readers was written from Turin, on the 19th of November, and is addressed to Sir Richard Lyttelton. Though he had been absent from England about five months, he had not then received a single letter, a circumstance which seems to have caused him some uneasiness, and which the letter-writing habits of the age among the higher classes renders the more remarkable:—

"MY DEAR SIR RICHARD,

"I am at length got over those impending precipices, covered with frozen snow, (that certainly Hannibal alone had the secret of melting with vinegar,) and repose myself now in the delicious plains of Italy. My eye has seen only what the French call the *affreuses beautés* of nature from Lyons quite to the Alps. I need not describe to you their horrible grandeur. But from the foot of Mount Cenis to Turin the lovely vale of Piedmont opens to you a thousand beauties, and all the *dolce* and *amabile* is laid before you.

"But I will not enter into minute descriptions of a country you have so lately seen, and will only in general tell you that I am much delighted with all I have seen, and liberally feast my imagination on the thoughts of what I am to see. I found every house open to me at Lyons, and everywhere the most polite and friendly reception. But I do not place this to my account, and I am pleased to tell my dear uncle the respect was shown to me as *to his nephew*; and there is nothing they would not do to oblige anybody you recommended.

"I have not yet received any letters from England. The silence of my friends I can attribute to a thousand accidental causes, from some of which they certainly proceed; *but Love will not be satisfied by Reason*, and ever suspects the worst. When you see my sweet girl, do, my dear uncle, tell her all my fears. I know the value of her too well not to be afraid of losing her. She is a treasure that multitudes long to possess. In my absence, every device will be conceived, and every means made use of, to deprive me of her. New lovers will be fired by her beauty, and importunities she will be forced to submit, though I hope, and rest assured, never to yield to. All that can make the ties of affection binding certainly has been used to make our love so, but time and absence may efface the tender impressions that early love has made upon her heart. Objections, too, may possibly arise, and *her parents*, and even my father, may possibly be inclined rather to divide than unite us. This, indeed, is to me a cruel consideration. 'Dark as I am, unconscious of their will,' I cannot prevent whatever may be done in my prejudice. I therefore stand much in need of one who loves me by inclination. I know of none who have given such proofs of love as you. To you, therefore, I apply, and entreat you to guard this fairer than Hesperian fruit. She will in everything be directed by you, and make you the confidant of her most secret thoughts. My lord she respects and loves, but she looks upon him as a father, and to him she fears to throw off all reserve.

"I am interrupted by a pacquet of letters from England—one from you, one from my father, and one from Miss Warburton. It always diminishes the pleasure I should have in hearing from you to see upon the superscriptions of your letters the doctor's hand. You say, my dear uncle, you have been ill ever since I left you. I hope only *ill with the gout*. Indeed, there is more vivacity in your letters than men generally have when they are oppressed with sickness. I trust, therefore, the pains in your hands and feet, though bad, are the worst you feel. I will leave you to think how sincerely I wish those pains were removed.

"Miss W.'s letter has removed all jealous suspicions of her constancy. She professes herself, in the language of desiring love, to be *mine, and only mine*. She has promised to send me her picture, and I will bid her deliver it to you as soon as it is painted. You will be so good as to order it to be enclosed in such a frame as will make it fit to be hung to my watch, and then will send it immediately to me. I believe I cannot have it before I get to Venice.

"I reflect with pleasure, my dear uncle, upon the conversations that passed between us at Richmond; and it is a great happiness to me that your inclinations and mine should be the same in points of so great importance to my future welfare.

"Ambitious, to you I confess myself to be, but I am also diffident of myself. I have something of the presumption, but all the heat, of youth about me. To your advice and direction I give up myself. Tempered and influenced by your judgment, my ambition may not be fruitless.

"I have wrote a long letter, and not said a word about Turin. The town, you know, is a fine one, and the society I am got into is very agreeable. The women, too, are most incitingly handsome. I am *cecisbeo*,[3] *en passant*, to her who I think is much the prettiest in the place. I shall set out to Milan in three days, or perhaps I may prolong it to a week. I told you in my last that Pernon was to supply me with all my clothes. I have found some at Turin much handsomer (and I think cheaper) than any he has got. I therefore intend to have only one *habit de galas* of him, and the other made here. Adieu.—I am ever your most dutiful nephew,

"T.L."

He proceeded from Turin to Venice, as indicated in the preceding letter; for in a subsequent letter he alludes to a gambling transaction in the latter city, which seems to have been the first incident of his tour which drew down upon him the reproaches of his father and uncle. It must not be forgotten, in justice to young Lyttelton, that the institutions and habits of Italian society at this period were not favourable to morality. Gambling and gallantry (as unbridled libertinism was then called, in the delicate phraseology of fashionable life) were the vices of the age; and in none of the European capitals were they more prevalent than in Turin and Florence. "Gambling," says Lady Morgan, "was the prevailing vice, from the king to the least of his courtiers. Pharobanks were publicly kept; jewels and trinkets were staked when all else was gone; and the enormous sums won from young English travellers at the court of Turin by the native nobility could not save them from ruin, brought on by play and by a total neglect of their affairs. The bond of marriage was one of mere accommodation. The necessity (originating in fashion) which every man was under of neglecting his own wife, and entering into the service of his neighbour's, while it undermined morality, deprived taste of its preference, and passion of its excitement; and general gallantry was so blunted by authorised libertinism that lovers became as stupidly loyal as husbands were confessedly faithless."[4]

There is no doubt that it was in Italy that the germs of the twin passions that dominated the life of Thomas Lyttelton were implanted. Between the letter from Turin and the next which I have before me—thick, gilt-edged post quarto, yellow with age, and the ink faded to a yellowish-brown hue—there is an interval of six months. In that period occurred the gambling loss at Venice, two duels at Bologna, and several affairs of gallantry with Italian women, which we shall find alluded to in a subsequent letter, but concerning which no details appear ever to have been known in England.

While at Bologna, or shortly after leaving that city, he wrote to Sir Richard Lyttelton an account of the circumstances connected with a duel in which he had there been engaged with an Italian gentleman; but it seems that his uncle thought that something had been withheld from him, and Thomas Lyttelton, in a letter written from Naples, on the 11th of May, 1764, while assuring him that he had withheld no circumstance connected with that affair, acknowledged that there had been another, at the same place, concerning which he had been silent, "because it happened with an Englishman who is too much my friend for me to let it be known that my honour obliged me to purchase a just satisfaction at his expense."

It appears from the statement which he wrote from Naples, that the Englishman, whose name was Pigott, had been at Eton with him, and that the quarrel out of which the duel arose occurred at a little dinner-party, given by himself, the other guests being two English artists, named Brumpton and Wilson. The conversation took a literary turn, and some difference of opinion arose between

Lyttelton and Pigott, which, owing probably to both being heated with wine, culminated in hasty and offensive words, followed by a challenge and a hostile encounter. Each of the parties regarded the other as the aggressor, and it is evident from Lyttelton's explanation that there was wrong on both sides, though the cause was so trivial that it might well have been adjusted by an exchange of apologies.

The gambling losses at Venice were, however, regarded as the most serious of young Lyttelton's follies, both by himself and the family. Sir Richard's purse-strings had again to be untied, and his nephew expressed the deepest gratitude for the relief. "Is it possible," he wrote, "for me to express by words the acknowledgments I owe you for your most noble and disinterested generosity to me? Henceforward, in every action of my life, I will endeavour to show the deep gratitude your unwonted kindness has raised in my heart. Guided and directed by you, to your opinion I submit everything that concerns me, and should hold myself unworthy to live if I disobliged you in any one instance, who have added to the strong ties of relationship the infinitely more strong ones of unbounded love. It is indeed the debt immense of endless gratitude still owing, still to pay.

"Nothing I can ever do can balance the account, but no future ill-conduct of mine shall, at least designedly, lower me in your opinion and affections. In respect to the cursed transaction that raised your just anger against me at Venice, I do give you the most solemn and sacred assurances that you have nothing to fear upon that account. Gaming I hold in detestation, and if again I ever relapse in that most absurd vice, I will forfeit my life, my estate, or what is as dear to me as either, the good opinion of men, and will allow myself patiently to be treated with universal contempt. Moderate play, too, when it is absolutely for amusement, I hold in great aversion, for, as I always either lose or am cheated out of my money, it is no amusement to me. Last night I lost thirty ounces at a game I thought it impossible to lose ten at; and at sober whist, at seven ounces the rubber, I lost seven rubbers together. So I have now determined never again (at least while I am abroad) to play, even for trifles. Of this you, *upon my honour*, may be as well assured as of my determination about gaming."

The next of the unpublished letters is undated, but was written from Toulon, probably in the latter part of 1764. The time was approaching for his return to England, and his union with Miss Warburton, for which he was as anxious as he had been before his departure. Though there is nothing in the published letters of his father to indicate the nature and extent of the causes of the displeasure with which he was regarded on his return to England, the rupture of the matrimonial treaty has generally been regarded as due to his misconduct while in Italy; but the following letter, addressed to Sir Richard Lyttelton, throws a new light on the subject, and, if it does not fully explain the cause of the rupture, exonerates the writer from the suspicion of having been the cause of it:—

"I have the pleasure to inform you that I have left Italy, though allowed by a charming woman to give some time more to the most delicious pleasures I have ever yet enjoyed. It is, indeed, a land of softness and delight. The women, like Armidas, have the power of fascinating their lovers, and of instilling into the most ambitious minds the love of ignoble ease and voluptuous refinement. But when the love of honour predominates they charm in vain. For myself, I can answer that I would as lief spend my days among the savages of wild America as in the arms of the most charming of the fair Italian ladies.

"I embarked last week with Lord Ossory from Genoa, and we purposed to continue our voyage, without stopping, towards Antibes. We were carried on by a very favourable wind to Hospitaletto, a little village about twenty miles from Monaco, when the wind suddenly changed, and we were forced to quit our feluccas, and continue our route upon mules to Monaco. We stayed there two days, and then, as the wind was fair, we again embarked. The sea, which had been agitated by violent storms, was much more swelled than we supposed, and the waves ran so high that we more than once expected to be overset. By good luck, however, we got to Villafranca, where we remained until the sea was quite calm, and from thence sailed most agreeably to Antibes.

"I write you this letter from Toulon. As the weather has been bad, I have not yet been able to see the port, which is the finest the French have in the Mediterranean, and where there are at this time twenty ships of the line.

"In the last letter I wrote to you, I desired *your directions* in respect to the future course of my travels. You well know the situation of my affairs in England. I am *betrothed* to a woman whom I would give the world to enjoy, and whom I cannot marry until those preliminaries are settled which *cannot be settled* until the General has sold his estate. *The estate is not sold*, as I know of, and my marriage is no farther advanced than it was a year and a half ago. To what purpose, then, should I return in so nice a conjuncture? The sight of my mistress will raise to an ungovernable height that desire of possessing her which the enjoyment of the finest Italian ladies has never been able to diminish.

"I love you, my dear uncle—I love you in my heart. I wish to live with you. I prefer Miss Warburton's love to that of any other woman; but, *in this crisis*, I had rather be *a banished man, condemned abroad to roam.* Time, that great artificer of men's fortunes, may work some lucky change. Her father is very old; he is turned of seventy. When the old man dies, she will have at once, and in her own power, a fortune of fifty thousand pounds. It is also probable he may sell the estate. He must some time or other find a purchaser. Was anything, in short, to happen that might facilitate this wished-for alliance, I would instantly direct my course to England; but till some preparatory step be taken, *I think I am better where I am,* improving myself by foreign observation and experience. I mean only for some months to come. Before the summer ends, I would, I think, at all events be in England; and by prolonging thus much my stay abroad, I gain many considerable advantages, and finish more completely this most useful part of my education. I propose these doubts *to you only*, and I beg, my dear uncle, you will not betray to anybody the unlimited confidence I have in your goodness and friendship. Write me soon an answer.— T. LYTTELTON.

"I beg you would excuse my ending so abruptly my letter, but I was led on unawares to the end of my paper. Accept my most grateful thanks for the thousand favours I have received from you, and believe me for ever attached to you. Direct *aux soins* of John Birkbeck, Esq., à Marseilles."

The projected marriage with Miss Warburton must have been broken off shortly afterwards, for on the 1st of January, 1765, his father wrote as follows: "My son is in France, where, I believe, he will stay till about the beginning of April. His match is off. If you will ask the reason, I can give it you in no better words than those of Rochefoucault, who says that *une femme est un bénéfice qui oblige à la résidence*." He adds, in another letter: "By his letters it appears that there is a great energy and force in his understanding; and as his faults are only those of most of our young travellers, I hope his return to England, and cool reflection on the mischief of his past follies, will enable his reason to get the better of any recent ill habits contracted by him already, and that his natural goodness of heart will give a right turn to the vivacity of his passions."[5] There is nothing in this extract to show that the tinge given to young Lyttelton's character by Italian manners and institutions was deeper than was usually contracted by young men on their travels; but it can scarcely be doubted that it was deeper than was then feared.

His resolution to avoid gambling was not abiding. The disappointment of the hope he had so long indulged with regard to Miss Warburton may have led him to seek the excitement of play as a means of diverting his mind from it; but he informed Sir Richard Lyttelton, in a letter from Dijon, dated the 15th of February, that it was an Italian, not an English lady, who had been the innocent cause of his moral aberration. He at first won largely, and then had a run of ill-luck, which obliged him to draw for £500 to satisfy his debts of honour, and for £250 for his expenses at Marseilles and Aix.

"I will not presume," he wrote, "by any excuse to endeavour to regain your favours and affection. I am sensibly enough convinced that I have the *very great misfortune* to have lost them *irrecoverably.* I shall always remember with most heartfelt gratitude the tenderness and confidence reposed in me by the most generous of parents. The debt I owe you is too immense ever to be repaid. In regard to the money I have spent, I will confess myself legally your debtor for all or any part of the sum. In times to come I may be able to discharge it."

His Continental tour had already been prolonged beyond the period originally fixed for it; and he did not return until the summer, when the first thing that we hear of him is the part he took in a masque at Stowe, for which he composed some tolerable verses, which were spoken by a little girl in the character of Queen Mab, and embodied a very graceful compliment to the character and abilities of the host, Earl Temple. With the exception of this pleasing little incident, the three years succeeding his return to England are a blank; but his letters show that, during at least a portion of this time, he was under the cloud of paternal displeasure and social proscription, the causes of which can only be inferred from the manner in which his candour invariably led him to speak of his own faults. The chronological arrangement of his letters can he determined only by internal evidence, which is often very slight or wholly deficient; but it appears from the eleventh of the series[6] that he was in the position described in the spring of 1768, and it was probably some time before that period that he wrote the following letter to a friend who had accused him of neglect, and reproached him with his failings:—

"MY DEAR FRIEND,

"You do me great injustice. I receive your letters with the greatest pleasure; and I gave your last the usual welcome, though every line was big with reproaches to me. I feel myself greatly mortified that you should have a suspicion of any neglect on my part. When I cease to answer your addresses you will be justified in supposing me careless about them: till then, you will, I hope, do me the justice, as far at least as relates to yourself, to think well of me. I very sensibly feel the advantage of your good opinion, and the loss of it would greatly affect me. You may be assured that my insensibility to reputation is not such as some part of my conduct may have given you reason to believe; for, after all his blustering and looking big, the heart of the worst man cannot be at ease, when he forces a look of contempt towards the ill opinion of mankind. In spite of all his bravadoes, he is a hypocrite twelve hours out of the four-and-twenty; and hypocrisy, as it is well said, is the homage which Vice pays to Virtue: unwillingly, I confess; but still she is forced to pay it.

"I will most frankly acknowledge to you that I have been as well disposed to turn my back upon the good opinion of the world as any one in it; and that I have sometimes accomplished this important business without confusion of face, but never without confusion of heart. On a late very mortifying occasion, it was not in my power to possess myself either with one or the other. At a public and very numerous meeting in the county where my father lives, where great part of his property lies, where his influence is considerable, and his name respectable, I was not only deserted, but avoided; and the women could not have discovered more horror on my approaching them if I had been Tarquin himself. I found myself alone in the crowd, and, which is as bad, alone out of the crowd. I passed the evening without company; and two or three such evenings would either have driven me to despair or have reformed me. I was then convinced, as I always am when I write to you, that there is some particle of good still remaining in me: but I flew from that solitary scene which gave such a conviction, to renew that dissolute intemperance which would destroy it.

"It is a great misfortune that vice, be it what it may, will find some one or other to flatter it; and that there should be assemblies of people, where, when public and honourable society has hissed you from the stage, you may find, not only reception, but applause—little earthly pandemoniums, where you meet with every means to hush the pains of reflection, and to guard against the intrusions of conscience. It requires a most gigantic resolution to suffer pain when passion quickens every sense, and every enticing object beckons to enjoyment. I was not born a Stoic, nor am I to be made a martyr. So much do I hate and detest pain, that I think all good must be dear that is to be purchased with it. Penitence is a rack where offences have been grievous. To sit alone and court reflection, which will come, perhaps, every moment, with a swinging sin at her back, and to be humble and patient beneath the stripes of such a scourge, by heavens, it is not in human nature to bear it! I am sure, at least, it is not in mine. If I could go to confession, like a good papist, and have the score wiped off at once, *à la bonne heure!* But to repent like a sobbing paralytic Presbyterian will not do for me; I am not fat enough to repent that way. George Bodens may be qualified for such a system of contrition, but my skinny shape will not bear mortification; and if I were to attempt the subdual of my carnal lust by fasting and prayer, I should be soon fasted and prayed into the family vault, and disappoint the worms of their meals.

"I have had, as you well know, some serious conversations with my father upon the subject and one evening he concluded a Christian lecture of a most unchristian length by recommending me to address Heaven to have mercy upon me, and to join my prayers to his constant and paternal ones for my reformation. These expressions, with his preceding counsels, and his affecting delivery of them, had such an effect upon me, that, like the king in Hamlet, I had bent the stubborn sinews of my knees, when it occurred to me that my devotions might be seen through the key-hole. This drew me from my pious attitude, and, having secured this aperture, so unfriendly to secret deeds, I thought it would not be an useless precaution to let down the window-curtains also; and, during the performance of that ceremony, some lively music, which struck up in the street, caught my attention, and gave a sudden flirt to all my devout ideas; so I girded on my sword, and went to the Little Theatre in the Haymarket, where Mrs. Cole and the Reverend Dr. Squintum soon put me out of humour with praying, and into humour with myself.

"I really began this letter in very sober seriousness; and, though I have strayed from my grave airs into something that wears a ludicrous appearance, I beg of you not to give up all hopes of my amendment. If there were but half-a-dozen people in the world who would afford me the kind encouragement I receive from you, it would, I verily believe, work a reformation in the prodigal; but the world has marked me down for so much dissoluteness as to doubt, at all times, of the sincerity of my repentance. —— has already told me, more than once, that I am got so deep into the mud as to make it highly improbable that I should ever get out; that I am too bad ever to be good; and that my future lot is either to be an open villain or an undeceiving hypocrite. Pretty encouragement, truly! Lady Huntingdon would tell me another story; but, however that may be, I shall never give myself up for lost while I retain a sense of your merit and a value for your friendship."

George Bodens, whose name appears more than once in the letters which must be frequently quoted in these memoirs, has not left his name on the records of the age; but that he was one of the associates, whose influence upon the character and career of Thomas Lyttelton was feared by the friends of the latter may be inferred from a letter written at a subsequent period by Earl Temple, and which will be given in its proper place.

There were probably alternate storms and calms in the relations between Lord Lyttelton and his scapegrace son, and the scene related in the foregoing letter must have taken place during one of the intervals of peace. Earl Temple seems always to have used his influence in his young relative's true interests; and his counsels had probably their due weight in the decision that was arrived at in 1767, that the family influence should be used to give the energies and abilities of Thomas Lyttelton an useful and honourable field for their exercise by obtaining him a seat in Parliament. At the ensuing general election he became a candidate for the representation of Bewdley, a little borough in which his family possessed considerable interest, and which had been represented by a Lyttelton on several previous occasions. Great exertions were made to secure his return, but he headed the poll by only a small majority over Sir Edward Winnington. He seems to have attached much importance to the attainment of this position, which would give him occupation, and open a career for him; but both himself and friends were again doomed to be disappointed.

1. *Quarterly Review*, December, 1851.
2. "Memoirs and Correspondence of George Lord Lyttelton." 1845.
3. *Chaperon* had been written here, but scored out with the pen.
4. "Italy," vol. i., p. 90.
5. "Memoirs and Correspondence of George Lord Lyttelton." 1845.
6. "Letters of the late Lord Lyttelton." 1806.

III

POLITICS OF THE PERIOD

FOR NEARLY HALF a century, from the change of dynasty which took place on the death of Queen Anne until the accession of George III, the government of this country had been almost constantly in the hands of the Whigs. Sir Robert Walpole, Pelham, the Duke of Newcastle, and the Earl of Chatham had all been taken from this party, which, as long as the national liberties seemed to be threatened by the pretensions of the Stuarts, had the support of the landed interest, as well as the sympathies of the trading and industrial classes. The cessation of this fear wrought a change in the policy of the Crown and the aristocracy. George III, who had the most exalted notions of the royal prerogative, showed, from the beginning of his reign, a strong desire to extend the power of the Crown and to keep that of the people within the strictest limits that the Constitution rendered possible; and hence the storm with which the Crown and its advisers were assailed from the first year of the Administration of the Earl of Bute down to the dawn of the era of Parliamentary reform. Grenville, who succeeded Bute in 1763, left the Wilkes prosecution and outlawry and the American Stamp Act as legacies to his successors, under whom they bore bitter fruit. The Stamp Act was repealed under the Whig Ministry formed by the Marquis of Rockingham, but the right to tax the colonies, which was the matter in dispute between them and the mother country, was reserved.

The Rockingham Administration did not long continue in power, being supplanted by the second Ministry of the Earl of Chatham, which was, however, less popular than the first. Indeed, all the Cabinets of this period suffered from the popular suspicion that they were composed of mere puppets, moved at the will of the Crown, and the strings of which were pulled by the Earl of Bute. The Earl of Chatham was, unfortunately, prevented by ill-health from taking an active part in the business of the State, and, on the death of Charles Townshend, who was, after the Premier, the most able member of the Cabinet, he resigned. Early in 1768, a new administration was formed by the Duke of Grafton, and a general election took place. Such was the state of affairs when Thomas Lyttelton entered Parliament as the representative of Bewdley.

John and George Damer sat in the same Parliament, the former for the now extinct borough of Gatton, and the latter for Cricklade. Another of his fellow-members was George Durant, who sat for Evesham, and of whose history and connection with the Lyttelton family we have the following account in a letter from Thomas Lyttelton to a friend:—

"Your usual accuracy has failed you in your suggestions concerning the rise and rapid progress of Mr. [Durant's] fortune. The history of that gentleman's advancement to his present affluence, if my immediate recollection does not fail me, is as follows: That he was appointed to his first employment in the service of Government by my father's interest is true; and it may, perhaps, have been procured for him from the motives which current opinion has assigned; but of this I do not pretend to be better informed than the rest of the world. Thus placed in a situation of little or no leisure, he was left, I believe, by our family patronage, to look for any future promotion from his own industry, the chance of succession, or the casual boon of fortune. The latter was disposed to smile upon him, or, it may be said with more propriety, to reward the prudent modesty with which he retreated from her first advances to secure her greater favours.

In the usual course of promotion he had an acknowledged claim to succeed to a vacant place of no inconsiderable profit. On this occasion Lord Holland, for some particular reason which I have forgotten, or perhaps never heard, wished to make an irregular appointment in favour of some other person; and, to comply with his lordship's wishes, Mr. [Durant] wisely waived his right of succession. That nobleman, who never suffered a good office to be long unreturned, soon after procured him to be named commissary-general to the expedition then preparing to attack the French West India islands. The success which attended it, together with the regular profits of his appointment, placed him in a situation, with respect to fortune, with which, it may be imagined, he was more than satisfied; and I have been told that he then looked no farther.

"But Lord Holland never thought he did enough for any one that had obliged him; and I am greatly mistaken if his influence did not name Mr. [Durant] to the same employment in the formidable armament which was sent against the Havannah, and succeeded. The fortunes acquired by that capture are well known, and Mr. [Durant's] was among the largest of them. On his return to England he soon began to display a love of ostentation, which he displayed, however, as I understand, without injuring his fortune; for, though George has no small share of vanity, it has seldom operated so far as to make him inattentive to the *summum bonum* of life. He built a fine house in Portman Square, and purchased the very capital estate of Tong Castle, in Shropshire, of the Duke of Kingston. He immediately renewed, or rather improved, the ancient form of the decayed edifice, adorned with the venerable decorations of Gothic architecture, beautified its surrounding lawns, and conducted through them a long extent of fine water, which flows on three sides of the stately edifice. The castle is a very large building, contains many very capacious apartments, and is furnished with a profusion of pictures and splendid upholstery. Though it is not situated in a fine part of the country, yet, taken in all its circumstances, it may lay no small claim to the character of magnificence. The owner of it might have built a new and more commodious house for much less money than has been expended in the reparations of the old one; but the word *castle* is a sounding word. It was in unison with Mr. [Durant's] notions of grandeur; and, apprehensive that this favourite title might, by degrees, be forgotten with the lofty turrets and stately battlements, he resolved to clothe them in more than pristine grandeur, and thus secure their ancient, honourable name, till time or chance should destroy them for ever. Some of my old neighbours positively assert that they remember to have heard George [Durant] declare, when he was a youth, that he hoped, one day or other, to be possessed of a larger house than Hagley; and they insist upon it that he gives such great extent to the limits of Tong Castle merely to fulfil his own prediction.

"But this by the way. The world in general, who were not acquainted with the ambition of his early days, have thought that by this creation of splendour he hoped to allure some lady of noble birth and great connections to become the mistress of it. The bait offered by so handsome a man as he certainly is would, in all probability, have been soon taken, but, in this particular, expectation has been very much disappointed, for he has actually made a kind of half-runaway match with a little Quaker of eighteen years of age, and educated in all the rigour of her sect. She has no pretension to beauty (I write merely from information), but possesses a very agreeable person, with a most amiable simplicity, and loves her husband to idolatry. I have heard your friend, Councillor Day, speak in high terms of her father, as a man of excellent understanding, polite manners, and generous disposition. Since this marriage, the superb service of plate very seldom makes its appearance; and the master of the noble castle, as I am told, now lives in a corner of it, with a small party of his relations, and seems to be growing into a disregard of the intrigues and fashions of public life. His brother[1] is the parson of my parish, and is called Doctor John; but the divine and the squire do not hold a very friendly intercourse.

"I rather think that this little piece of biography is pretty well founded: if, however, it should possess any errors, I beg leave to assure you that they are not of my invention. As to Mr. [Durant's] unpopularity with the Lyttelton family, it does not arise, perhaps, from what you and the world may, with some reason, suppose; but from a subsequent circumstance, of which you and the world are, in general, ignorant. When my [uncle] was governor of [Jamaica] he received positive orders to raise and discipline a regiment of negroes for the service of the Havannah expedition. As this supply did not join the grand armament at the time appointed, Mr. [Durant] was despatched to Jamaica by the commander-in-chief, to chide the tardy levies; and, as report says, he found a very surprising languor in obeying these very important orders of Government. On such an occasion he was, perhaps, instructed to threaten an accusation of delinquency against the governor to the powers at home; and it is equally probable that he did not forget his instructions. Whether this neglect was repaired by subsequent exertions, or whether it was forgotten in the successes which followed, I do not know; but I very well remember that at the time my father was very uneasy about it, and complained, in angry terms, to the clergyman of Hagley of his brother's forwardness to disgrace a branch of that family by which his own had been so warmly protected. Here the matter rested; but that George [Durant] should have been elevated to a situation wherein he could repeat what was called an insolent menace to one of the Lyttelton family will never be remembered without much mortification, and therefore can never be forgiven. Adieu."

This letter, with its revelations of irregular appointments and fortunes made by commissaries-general under a corrupt system of Government, constitutes an appropriate commentary on the results of that condition of the representative institutions of the country of which we have illustrations in the existence of such constituencies as Gatton and Old Sarum, and the return of such men as the Damers by means which were no secret. The return of Thomas Lyttelton was petitioned against, on the ground of fraud, it being alleged that recourse had been had to the system of manufacturing "occasional burgesses," in order to secure his election. But it is probable that he was quite as much the choice of the electors of Bewdley as the majority of the members of the Commons' House of Parliament at that day were of the constituencies of which they were the ostensible representatives.

Parliament assembled on the 10th of May, and on the 18th Thomas Lyttelton delivered his maiden speech, the occasion being one of the many stormy debates that arose out of the case of John Wilkes, of *North Briton* and *Essay on Woman* notoriety. Not a line of this first oratorical effort is to be found in "Hansard," but we learn from the meagre sketch of it in the "Cavendish Debates," that the line of argument adopted by the speaker was, that it was unwise to bestow so much time upon such an insignificant subject, when the American colonies were so disturbed on account of the fiscal measures of the late Administration, and a strong Government was so obviously and imperatively required. The speech made a favourable impression upon the House, and elicited a compliment from Wellbore Ellis, who observed that the honourable member for Bewdley had spoken with hereditary ability.

The compliment was sweet incense to the family foible; and its occasion brought about a temporary reconciliation between young Lyttelton and his offended relatives. The truce was as brief, however as the future orator's possession of his seat. The Committee to which the petition against his return was referred reported unfavourably to him; and, on the 28th January, 1769, he was declared not to have been duly elected, and the seat was transferred to Sir Edward Winnington.

It was at this time that the celebrated letters of "Junius" began to attract that large share of public attention which they received during several years, and which has, from time to time, been directed to them from that period to the present day, through the efforts which have been made to fix the identity of their author. Three-quarters of a century afterwards, an attempt[2] was made to assign the authorship of these famous letters to Thomas Lyttelton, on the ground of certain expressions and turns of thought which are found both in the letters of "Junius" and in those of Lyttelton, and others which, in the opinion of the writer, favour the hypothesis that Woodfall's mysterious correspondent was "a dissolute young man." Wade had just taken equal pains to prove that "Junius" could have been neither a peer nor a member of the House of Commons; but, without entering into the often-discussed question as to who "Junius" really was, it will be sufficient here to show that there are very small grounds for identifying him with Thomas Lyttelton.

The similarities of thought and expression which are found in the letters of "Junius" and in those of Lyttelton are not remarkable enough to warrant the inference that the two sets of correspondence emanated from the same mind and hand. Most of them are coincidences which are almost certain to occur to any two writers of the same period, regarding the same topics from the same point of view, or from similar points; and though, unfortunately for his memory, it cannot be contended that Thomas Lyttelton was not a dissolute young man, there were so many young men of the same character, in and out of Parliament, who were contemporary with "Junius," that dissolute habits can scarcely be regarded as a characteristic by which the authorship of the letters in the *Advertiser* can be assigned to him. He was only twenty-four years of age when the letters signed "Junius" began to appear, and, though he had given considerable attention to the political questions of the day during the short period that he sat in the House of Commons, and, in the words of the author of the theory under consideration, "those who knew him intimately discerned very early the superiority of his genius, and gave him credit, while yet plunged in profligacy, for qualities which would conduct him to eminence, should he ever resolve on doing justice to himself he can scarcely have possessed the experience and knowledge of public affairs evinced by "Junius."

In order to account for "the profound knowledge and matured political opinion he displayed on his first appearance" in the House of Lords, and to explain the "confidence in his powers that distinguished his speeches, and surprised even more than his eloquence," the writer in the *Quarterly Review* states that, "for seven years previous to his father's death he studiously shrouded his motions, frequently concealing his residence from his friends," and infers "that that time—despite profligate habits—must have been spent in intellectual exercises." That much of the time referred to was thus creditably and profitably employed, there is abundant evidence in his letters and speeches to prove; but the fact does not help us very far to the conclusion that he was "Junius."

Seven years previous to the death of his father carries us back to the summer of 1766, one year after his return from his Continental tour, and when he was in his twenty-second year. In 1768 he was in Parliament, and he seems, during the short time that he held his seat, to have given an exemplary attention to his legislative duties. There is not much data as to the manner in which the next three years were spent, but he was at Ghent in 1769, and in Italy during the following year; and it seems probable that he left England for a second Continental tour soon after he lost his seat in Parliament, and remained abroad until the end of 1771, or the beginning of 1772.

The misty veil that conceals his movements during the interval is explicable without recourse to the supposition that he withdrew from the world for the purpose of forging in retirement the weapons of future political controversy. His public career had received a check that had disappointed himself equally with his friends, and he was, besides, under the ban of paternal and family displeasure. No one was concerned as to where he was or what he was doing. Hence it is that there is not a line about him—not the merest mention of his name—either in the letters of his father or in those of his noble relative, the Earl of Chatham. What his relations with his family were at this time can be seen from two letters written shortly before his return to England, and the first of which is as follows:—

"So [George Ayscough] turns up his eyes and significantly shrugs his shoulders when my name is mentioned, and, to continue the farce, pretends to lament me as a disgrace to his family! I am almost ashamed to acknowledge it, but this idle history has given me a more stinging mortification than I almost ever felt. How insignificant must he become who is openly despised by insignificance! and how loud must the hiss of the world be when such a puny whipster insults me! If honourable men were to speak of me with contempt, I should have submitted without resentment, for I have deserved it. If they should bestow their pity upon me, I should thank them for giving me more than I deserve. If mankind despise, I have only to resist, or fly from the contempt; but to be an object of supercilious airs from one who, two years ago, would have wiped the dust from off my shoes, and who, perhaps, two years hence will be proud of the same office—a puny prattler, who does not possess a sufficient degree of talent or importance to give dignity either to virtue or crime—I say to be the butt of such a one severely mortifies me. Were I on the other side of the water, his back-biting looks and shrugs should be changed in a moment to well-made bows and suppliant postures. If I live, the scurvy knave shall do me homage! It really frets me that I cannot in four-and-twenty hours meet him face to face, and make his subservient attentions give the lie to his humbling compassion in the presence of those before whom he has traduced me. The day of my revenge will come, when he shall open his mouth for me to spit in it, as he was wont to do, and perform every dirty trick for which parasites were formed. His genius is to fetch and carry—a very spaniel, made to fawn and eat your leavings, whose whole courage rises no higher than to ape a snarl. If I live to outlive this sniffling pedagogue, I shall see him make a foolish end of it. Mark my words, I am a very Shylock, I will have Revenge!

"The last word I have written puts me in mind of telling you that —— has been with me for some time. The rascal, who is a priest into the bargain, carried *aqua fortis* in a syringe for three months together, to squirt the fiery liquor into the eyes of a fortunate rival. In this diabolical design he succeeded, and the object of his malice was for ever deprived of half his sight. I have conversed with him on the horrors of this transaction, but the Italian finds a consolation in his own infernal feelings, and a justification in the dying commands of his father, whose last words composed this emphatic sentence: 'Remember, my son, that revenge is sweet!'

"This man is capable of any villainy, if money is to be got by it; and I doubt not but he might be bribed to undertake, without hesitation, robbery, seduction, rape, and murder. However, my superior virtue for once overawed his villainy; for he most certainly had it in his power to have robbed me of a large sum of money without the possibility of a discovery, and, if he thought it necessary, he might have despatched me with as little danger. I have since asked him what strange fit of virtue or fear of the devil came across him when he had such an opportunity to make his fortune? The impudent rascal replied at once that he had very powerful suggestions to send me to the other world, and that if, fortunately for him, I had possessed one single virtue, he should, without ceremony, have despatched me to my reward. This event will, I think, make a complete Mandevillian of me. You see, for your encouragement, that a bad life is good for something; and for the good example which the world will receive from me in times to come, it will be indebted to the very bad one I have already given it. After this signal and providential preservation, I cannot but think that Heaven has something particularly great in store for me.

"As I tell it you, this history has the air of a *badinage*, but you may be assured that it is a real fact, and I am sorry that the circumstances of it are too long and various to be inserted in a letter. I believe you know something of the man, but if you repeat what I have written to any one who is acquainted with him, you will soon find that I have had a very narrow escape. I have bribed him to leave me, and he is gone for England. The story of Lewis the Fourteenth and his barber is well known, and you may, if you please, apply it to your affectionate," &c.

George Edward Ayscough was the son of the Rev. Dr. Francis Ayscough, who had been tutor to Lyttelton's father at Oxford, and afterwards married Anne Lyttelton, the peer's sister, and became Dean of Bristol. George was, therefore, Thomas Lyttelton's cousin, and held a lieutenant's commission in the First Regiment of Foot Guards. That in the foregoing letter, and in the one that follows, he has not been misrepresented, is shown by the manner in which he is treated by Nichols. "It is painful," says that author, "to reflect on the miscarriages of families, or the profligacy of individuals; yet truth obliges me to observe, that the honour of the respectable house of Lyttelton derives little advantage from the conduct of this unhappy member of it. Though a military man, he submitted to be insulted by a gentleman[3] who repeatedly treated him as a poltroon; and, though in no affluent circumstances, he gave up his commission, to avoid doing his duty when called upon by his Sovereign to fight in America."[4] What Nichols says of his vicious and debauched conduct, may for the present be omitted. That it was to him the following letter was addressed, there can be no doubt:—

"You have certainly given yourself very unjustifiable airs upon my subject: neither your talents, knowledge, figure, courage, nor virtue, afford you the shadow of that superiority over me which, I understand, you affect to maintain. However imprudent or bad my conduct may have been; whatever vices I may unfortunately possess, be assured I do not envy you your snivelling virtues, which are worse than the worst vices, and give an example of meanness and hypocrisy in the extreme. Your letter is a *farrago* of them both; and since the receipt of it I despise you more than ever.

"What, sir? Has my father got a cough, or does he look thinner than usual, and read his Bible? There must be some certain symptoms of his decay and dissolution that could induce you to address yourself kindly to one who, to use your own expression, is, as he ought to be, abandoned by his family. You have dreamed of an hatchment upon Hagley House, and seen a visionary coronet suspended over my brow. You are a simpleton and a parasite to let such weak reasons guide you to wag your tail and play the spaniel, and renew your offers to fetch and carry. Be assured, for your comfort, that, if ever you and I have any future intercourse together, it will be upon such terms, or worse.

"I have heard it said, and I believe it to be true, that you pretend to lament your poor uncle's fate, and, with a more than rueful visage, prognosticate the breaking of his heart from the wicked life of his graceless son. Now, I will tell you a secret, that, supposing such a canting prophecy should take place to-morrow, you would be the first to flatter the *parricide*. I consider you with a mixture of scorn and pity, when I see you so continually pampered in difficulties from your regard to the present and future Lord: though you order your matters tolerably well, for there is not one of our family to whom your hypocritical canting will not answer in some degree, but to myself. I know you, and I declare you to be incapable of love or affection to any one, even to a mother or a sister. You know what I mean; but to quit an idea abhorrent to human nature, let me entreat you, if it is in your power, to act with candour, and, if you must speak of me, tell your sentiments openly, and not with those covert looks and affected shrugs, which convey so much more than meets the ear: and be so good, I pray you, as to raise your merit upon your own mighty stock of virtues, and not upon my vices. The world will one day judge between us, and I must desire you to be content with the acknowledged superiority you will receive from the arbitration in your favour.

> "*Oh, stultum nimis est, cum tu pravissima tentes,*
> *Altertius censor ut vitiosa notes!*

"I have not yet sung a requiem to my own honour; and, though you and some others of my good friends may have chaunted a dirge over the grave you have yourselves dug for it, it does not rest, however, without the hopes of a joyful and speedy resurrection. To have done with you for the present, I have only to desire you to be an open enemy to me, or a real friend, if you are capable of either; the halting between two opinions on the matter is both disgraceful and contemptible. Be assured that I give you these counsels more for your own sake than for that of your humble servant,

"[Thomas Lyttelton.]"

It is probable that Lyttelton, leaving England in disgrace with his family, and almost an outcast from reputable society, left debtors unsatisfied; and that to this circumstance must be ascribed the attempt to conceal his movements on his return, which elicited the friendly remonstrance to which the following letter is a reply, and which seems to constitute the slender foundation upon which the writer in the *Quarterly Review* built up the theory that he secluded himself from the world to study politics and write letters to the *Advertiser*:—

"You accuse me of neglect in not informing you that I was in London. Believe me, I had every disposition in the world to do it, but was opposed by circumstances, which, among other mortifications, prevented me from seeing you. I came to England in so private a manner that I imagined no one would, or, indeed, could know of my arrival; but, by a combination of unlucky circumstances, the secret was discovered, and by those who were the most likely to make a very unpleasant use of their knowledge. I was, therefore, obliged to shift my plan, and to beg H—— to give me an asylum in his house, where he very kindly received and entertained me. My abode was not suspected by any one; and I remained there till certain people were persuaded that I had never left the Continent, or was again returned to it; and till the hell-hounds which were in pursuit of me had relaxed their search.

"You must certainly have heard me mention something of my host and hostess; they are the most original couple that ever were paired together, and their singularity effected what, I believe, no other amusement could have attained—it made me forget the disagreeableness of my situation. He possesses a strange, wild, rhapsodic genius, which, however, is not uncultivated; and, amid a thousand odd, whimsical ideas, he produces original bursts of poetry and understanding that are charming. She is a foreigner, assumes the title of countess, and, without knowing how to write or read, possesses, in the circumstances of dress, behaviour, &c., all her husband's dispositions. She is fantastic, grotesque, *outré,* and wild; nevertheless, at times, there are very pleasing gleams of propriety in her manners and appearance.

"I cannot describe so well as you may conceive the striking and odd contrast of these two characters, and what strange sparks are produced by the collision of them. When she imagines that Cytherea acknowledges her divinity, and he grasps in his hand the lyre of Apollo; when the goddess unfolds herself to view with imaginary millions at her feet, and when the god chides the chairs and tables for not being awakened into a cotillion by his strains; in short, when the sublime fit of madness is on, it is an august scene; but if the divinities should rival each other, heaven changes instantly to hell, Venus becomes a trull, and Phœbus a blind fiddler. It is impossible to describe the riot; not only reflections, but things of a more solid nature are thrown at each other. Homer's genius is absolutely necessary to paint celestial combats. But it ends not here: this superb opera, which was acted at least, during my stay, three times a week, and rehearsed generally every day, for the most part has a happy conclusion. The contest requires the support of nectar, which softens the edge of resentment, puts the parties in good humour, and they are soon disposed to acknowledge each other's merit and station, with a zeal and fondness superior, if possible, to their late rage and opposition. A number of collateral circumstances serve as interludes to the grand piece, and though less sublime, are not less entertaining.

"You will now, probably, be no longer displeased with me for making my hiding-place a secret. One hour's attendance upon our orgies would have done for you; on the contrary, they suited me. I wanted something to hurry my spirits, to dissipate my thoughts, and amuse my mind; and I found it in this retreat. You know enough of the parties to enter into my description. I hope it will make you laugh; but, if my pen should fail, I will promise to make your sides ache when we meet again, a pleasure which I look to with a most sensible impatience."

He had not, it may be safely assumed, passed the period of his second Continental sojourn in scenes or with companions conducive to moral amendment. For ever making resolutions for the future, which he had not firmness enough to keep, he returned to England in a state of mind which forcibly illustrates the Zoroastrian creed, the powers of good and evil contending for mastery over the heart of man, and each in turn gaining the advantage over the other. Weary of his wandering life, surfeited with sensual pleasures, disgusted with the degradation of his surroundings, feeling with all the bitterness of his passionful nature his exclusion from the family circle, and from the society of his best friends, he came back to England with contrition on his lips; and who shall say that it was not in his heart? But at the bottom of that mysterious well-spring of human passions were pride and vanity, and an inordinate love of pleasure—the pride of intellect, the love of power, the thirst for applause, the worship of the flesh; all these, cast down for the moment, were ready to spring up and renew the struggle with every better feeling of the heart, every higher aspiration of the soul.

1. Rev. John Durant, D.D., Vicar of Hagley.
2. *Quarterly Review*, December, 1851.
3. Swift, author of a poem entitled "The Gamblers."
4. "Literary Anecdotes of the Eighteenth Century."

IV

FAMILY RELATIONS

THERE CAN BE no doubt that Thomas Lyttelton returned to England with a sincere desire for restoration to the family relations, which, by various circumstances, had been ruptured. He wrote to the principal members of his family, expressing regret for his past misconduct, assuring them of his contrition, and asking for their intercession with others on his behalf. Only one of these letters has been preserved.[1] It was probably addressed to Earl Temple, and is as follows:—

"It is so long since I received your letter that I am almost ashamed to answer it; and be assured that, in writing my apology, and asking your pardon, I act with a degree of resolution that I have seldom experienced. I hardly expect that you will receive the one, or grant the other. I do not deserve either, or indeed any kindness from you of any sort, for I have been very ungrateful. I am myself very sensible of it, and very much apprehend that you will be of the same opinion. I was never more conscious of my follies than at this moment; and if you should have withdrawn yourself from the very few friends which are left me, I shall not dare to complain; for I deserve the loss, and can only lament that another and a deeper shade will be added to my life. The very idea of such a misfortune is most grievous; and nothing can be more painful than the reflection of suffering it from a fatal, ill-starred, and abortive infatuation, which will prove my bane. I have written letters, since I received yours, to many who have never done me any kindness, to some who have betrayed me, and to others whose correspondence administered no one comfort to my heart, or honour to my character; and for them, at least engaged with them, I have neglected you, to whose disinterested friendship I am so much indebted, and which is now become the only point whereon to fix my anchor of hope.

"But this is not all; if it were, I have something within me which would whisper your forgiveness; for you know of what frail materials I am made; and have ventured, in the face of the world's malice, to prognosticate favourably of my riper life. But I fear that you will think meanness added to ingratitude when I tell you that I am called back to acknowledge your past goodness to me, and to ask a repetition of it, not from any renewed sentiment of honour or gratitude, but by immediate and wringing distress. in such a situation your idea presented itself to me—an idea which was not encouraged in seasons of enjoyment: it never wished to share my pleasure, but, like the first-born of friendship, it hastened to partake my pain. Though it came in so lovely a form, I dared not bid it welcome; and I started, as at the sight of one whom I had severely injured, whose neglect, contempt, and revenge I might justly dread, while I did not possess the least means of resistance, nor had a covert left where I might fly for refuge.

"This is a very painful confession, and will, I hope, plead my cause in your bosom, and win you to grant my request. I have written to —— for some time past, and have never been favoured with one line of reply. Indeed, it has been hinted that he refuses to read my letters. However that may be, he most certainly does not answer them. In order, therefore, that I may know my fate and be certain of my doom, I most earnestly and submissively entreat you to deliver the enclosed letter into his hands. If I should be deserted by you both, the consequences may be of such a nature as, in the most angry paroxysm, you would neither of you wish to your most obliged," &c.

It is doubtful whether the person mentioned in this letter as not answering his appeal was his father or Sir Richard Lyttelton, and the blanks in the next epistle throw no light upon the point. The latter was evidently addressed to a friend who was entirely in his confidence, the previous commission referred to in the first sentence relating to inquiries which he had asked his correspondent, while in Paris, to make concerning a lady whom he had met there. He respected the lady as much as he admired her, but he says that, of ten calls he had made upon her, he had been admitted only thrice, "when there was a great deal of company. This," he continues, "is a very superior woman; for, while she conducts herself in such a manner towards me as to tell me plainly, that the respect she has for my family is the only inducement to give me the reception she does, there is not a single look suffered to escape her from which any person might form the most distant suspicion of her sentiments concerning me." He had been unable, from indisposition, to bid her farewell in person, and had consoled himself "by writing her a letter, which was half serious, more than half gallant, and almost sincere." He wished to know whether, and in what manner, the lady had spoken of him; but his friend had been unable to learn, and Lyttelton thought it probable that his epistle had been consigned to the fire-grate.

"I have another commission for you, in which I flatter myself you will be more successful than in your last. You must know, then, that I am in a bad plight, and there is no good ground of expectation that matters will go better with me: on the contrary, the prospect is a dark one, and the gloom increases every step I take. To extricate myself, if possible, I wrote to ——, who has not answered my letters, and, I am disposed to think, never opens them. I was, therefore, under the necessity of addressing a very pitiful, penitential epistle to ——. I have used him scurvily, and made such an ill return to all his zeal to serve me, that I have too much reason to apprehend his resentment. He passed through —— about six weeks ago, without inquiring after me. However, without appearing to know anything of that circumstance, I ventured to tell a miserable tale to him, and to beseech his kindness would once more interest itself in my behalf, by delivering a letter into ———'s own hands. It would be an easy matter, I should imagine, to discover if he has complied with my request. T—— will inform you if he has been lately, and when, in —— Street. Perhaps he may have scented out something more; and whatever you can discover I should be glad to know with all possible despatch. They will probably be slow in their operations, whatever they may be; and your information will direct my hopes, or confirm my fears,—will either give a sunshine to the present shade, or prepare me for the worst."

He seems to have been some time in London before his return was known to the family, for Lord Chatham, in a letter to his father,[2] speaks of his return and the reconciliation as events more nearly connected in point of time than they appear to have been. The letter is dated February 16, 1772, and is as follows:—

"MY DEAR LORD,—The sincere satisfaction I feel on what I hear of Mr. Lyttelton's return, with all the dispositions you could wish, will not allow me to be silent on so interesting an event. Accept, my dear Lord, my felicitations upon these happy beginnings, together with every wish that this opening of light may ripen into the perfect day. I know what it is (thank God!) to be happy hitherto in my children; and I grieve for those who meet with essential disappointment in that vital part of domestic happiness. May you never again know anguish from such a wound to your comfort, but the remainder of your days derive as much felicity from the return as you suffered pain from the deviation."

Lord Lyttelton replied to these felicitations and good wishes as follows: "I give you a thousand thanks for your very kind felicitations on the return of my son, who appears to be returned, not only to me, but to a rational way of thinking, and a dutiful conduct, in which if he perseveres, it will gild with joy the evening of my life."

There are letters which appear to have been written by Thomas Lyttelton about this time, which afford further insight into his strangely compounded character, and throw light upon the causes of his long estrangement from his family. "There is nothing," he says in one of them, "so miserable, and, I may add, so unfortunate, as to have nothing to do. The peripatetic principle, that Nature abhors a vacuum, may be applied, with great propriety, to the human intellect, which will embrace anything, however criminal, rather than be without an object. It is a matter of indubitable certainty with me that, if I had kept my seat in Parliament, most of the unpleasant predicaments in which I have been involved since that time would have been avoided. I was disposed to application in the political line, and was possessed of that ready faculty of speech which would have enabled me to make some little figure in the senate. I should have had employment; my passions would have been influenced by a proper animating object, and my vanity would have been sufficiently satisfied. During the short time I sat in Parliament, I found myself in the situation I have described: I was pleased with the character; I availed myself of its privileges while I possessed them; I mingled in public debate, and received the most flattering testimonies of applause. If this scene had continued, it would have been very fortunate for myself, and have saved my friends great anxiety and many alarms: you, among the rest, would have been spared the pain of much unavailing counsel and disregarded admonitions.

"You know me well enough to be certain that I must have a particular and not a common object to employ my attention; it must be an object which inspires desire, calls forth activity, keeps hope upon the stretch, and has some sort of high colouring about it. Power and popular reputation are of this kind, and would greatly have engrossed my thoughts and wishes; they would have kept under the baser passions; I should have governed them at least; and my slavery, if I was destined to be a slave, would have been more honourable. But, losing a situation so suitable to me, I fell back, a prey to that influence which had already proved so fatal, and yielded myself a victim to an habitual dissoluteness which formed my only pleasure.

"I do not mean to write a disrespectful thought of my father; I would not offend you by doing it; but, surely, his ignorance of mankind is beyond all conception. It is hardly credible that a man of his understanding and knowledge, whose life has been ever in the world, and the most polished societies of it, who writes well and ably on its manners, should be so childish in its concerns as to deserve the coral that amused, and the go-cart that sustained him sixty years ago. I write in confidence, and you know what I assert to be true. Indeed, I might go further, and trace the errors of my own life from the want of that kind of paternal discernment which sees into the character of his child, watches over its growing dispositions, gently moulds them to his will, and completes the whole by placing him in a situation suitable to him.

"I have been the victim of vanity, and the sacrifice of me was begun before I could form a judgment of the passion. You will, probably, understand me; but if there should be the least gloom in my allusions, I will, with your leave, explain the matter more clearly in some future letter. There is a great deal of difference between a good man and a good father. I have known bad men who excelled my father as much in parental care as he was superior to them in real virtue. But more of this hereafter."

He continued the subject in the letter from which extracts are given in the first and second chapters of these memoirs, and which concludes as follows:—

"You know as well as myself what happened during my travels, as well as after my return; and I trust that you will impute my misconduct, in part at least, to its primary cause.

"In this short sketch of the matter, which consists rather of hints than descriptions, you will see the drift of my reasoning, and know how to apply it to a thousand circumstances in your remembrance. You were present at my being received into the arms of my family with a degree of warmth, delight, and triumph, which the brightest virtue could alone have deserved; and you recollect the cause of all this rapturous forgiveness, which, I believe, penitence itself would not, at that time, have effected; it was my having made a speech in Parliament, flowery, indeed, and bold, but very little to the purpose, and at a time when, as I was certain that I should lose my seat, it would have been prudent in me to have remained silent. However, Mr. Ellis thought proper to compliment me up the occasion, and to observe that I spoke with hereditary abilities; and this circumstance instantly occasioned the short-lived family truce that succeeded.

"That my relations may have cause to complain of me, I do not deny; but this confession is accompanied with an opinion, in which I doubt not of your acquiescence, that I, on my side also, have no small cause of complaint; and, however black the colour of my future life may be, I shall ever consider that the dusky scenes of it are occasioned by the vanity of my family, and not by any obdurate or inflexible dispositions inherent in my own character."

He had written at this time two "Dialogues of the Dead," one between Jesus and Socrates, the other between David and Cæsar Borgia, from hints given him at Turin by a free-thinking Frenchman. They are said to have been extremely irreverent and profane; but the suspicion that they were intended to ridicule the similar compositions of his father is declared by him to be without foundation.

"Bad as they may be," he observes, "they were not writ for so bad a purpose; and, if I had considered the possibility of such an idea becoming prevalent, they would never have been exposed to inspection. I wrote them originally in French, and never, to my recollection, gave them an English dress, but when I read them to some one who did not understand the former language. I was flattered into the suffering of some copies to be taken by the declaration of a respectable literary company that they were superior to Voltaire's tragedy of *Saul*; and these copies must have been greatly multiplied to have made it possible that one of them should have reached you. I am very sorry for it; for you have already more than sufficient reason to fill your letters to me with reproaches, and I to curse the chance that has thrown another motive in your way to continue a train so disagreeable to us both.

"It is true that my father is a Christian, and has given an ample testimony of his faith to the world by his writings; but it was long after he attained to my age that he became a convert to that system which he has defended. It is painful to me, and hardly fair in you, to occasion our being brought together in the same period; it takes from me the means of justification where I could use them, and of palliation where a complete defence might not be practicable. As to my right reverend uncle, I shall consider him with less ceremony. He also may be a good Christian; but I recollect to, have heard him make a better discourse upon the *outside* ornaments of an old Gothic pulpit—I think it was at Wolverhampton—than he ever delivered *in* one throughout the whole course of his evangelical labours. He seems much more at home in a little harangue on some doubtful remnant of a Saxon tombstone than in urging the performance of Christian duties, or guarding, with his lay brother, the Christian fortress against infidel invasion. I well remember, also, to have heard his right reverence declare that he would willingly give one of his fingers (that was his expression) to have a good natural history of Worcestershire. What holy ardour he may possess as an antiquarian, I cannot tell; but, in my conscience, I think he would make a sorry figure as a Christian martyr, and that a zeal for our holy religion would not inflame him to risk the losing of a nail from his finger.

"I repeat to you, upon my honour, that I did not wish these *jeux d'esprit* should have gone beyond the limits I had prescribed for them. The very few persons to whom I gave them were bound, by a very solemn promise, not to circulate their contents or to name their author. If they have forfeited their word, I am sorry for it; but the failure of their engagement cannot be imputed to me, and the severest judge would not think me guilty of more than chance-medley on the occasion. In your breast, I hope there is a complete and full acquittal for your most sincere and obliged," &c.

This letter, and others, show that he had read many of the deistical works of the period, and that he was suspected of having imbibed the sceptical views of revealed religion which were then beginning to pervade all classes of society in every civilised country. He is credited, however, in a passage of one of Pennington's works, which has been quoted by almost every subsequent writer by whom he has been mentioned,[3] with "a strong sense of religion;" and such a sentiment is not incompatible, as some of the most celebrated divines of the present day have shown, with views of the divine inspiration and literal interpretation of the Scriptures which, a century ago, were considered inconsistent with the belief of a Christian. Thomas Lyttelton, whatever else he was, was not a hypocrite; and his letters and speeches must be accepted, therefore, as evidence that he never ceased to be a Christian, though he may have had reasonable doubts upon some matters which it was then held to be impious to doubt. He lived in an age of active thought, when the minds of all who were capable of thinking were, at some period of their lives, more or less disturbed, as even his father's had once been, as he acknowledged on his death bed to Dr. Johnstone.[4]

The revolt of the intellect against old forms of religious belief was accompanied by a corresponding movement against the restraints of custom and convention, and society was threatened with the loss of its cohesion. It was heaving already with the coming throes of revolution. Young men like Thomas Lyttelton, endowed with active intellects and ardent temperaments, breaking the chains which had bound the minds of past generations, were dazzled by the illumination into which they rushed, and groped about as blindly as those who remained in the dark. They found the fences and landmarks of the moral world thrown down, and they wandered about in it, without guides, scoffing at warnings of their danger, and absorbed in the triumphs of the intellect and the pleasures of the senses.

It is impossible to understand the character of Thomas Lyttelton, and to do justice to it, without understanding the character of the age in which he lived. It was not a religious age; still less was it a moral age. The evidence afforded by contemporary memoirs, letters, and journals is conclusive upon this point. Religion was dead, morality at the lowest ebb; and the creeds, customs, and conventionalities which are their mere husk, and which alone remained, and passed current for them, were everywhere struggling to maintain themselves against the rising tide of new ideas. There was necessarily a large amount of hypocrisy in the world; for an outward reverence for religion and regard for morality was enforced by the example of the Court, and self-interest was a potent agent in prompting men who cared nothing about either to be loud in their professions of attachment to the Church, and unquestioning belief in the Articles of Religion.

Thomas Lyttelton was at least no hypocrite; whatever his other faults may have been, he was one of the most candid of mankind. "Open and ingenuous in his disposition," says one who knew him well,[5] "he soon became disgusted at the hypocrisy of mankind. … Less cautious in his amours than a more prudent, though not less guilty, man would be, it is not at all extraordinary that his lordship should have met with obloquy and reproaches, since there is no situation in life which will admit of an avowed contempt of vulgar prejudices." In several of his letters he attributes his bad reputation to these features of his character; and no one who has studied it, and the times in which he lived, can doubt that many worse men have enjoyed a better repute, simply because they took more care to seem better than they were, and put on the semblance of a piety and a virtue which they did not really possess.

"The world at large," says he, in a letter to a friend, "is so disposed to generalise, that it is seldom right when it descends into the detail of opinion. It has so many eyes and objects that, in the act of particularising the sources of its favour or disapprobation, the rectitude or error of its conclusions are both the effect of hazard. I, as you too well know, have been the subject of its severest censure; but, with all my faults, I have much reason to complain of its precipitate injustice.

"Among other instances of its premature indisposition towards me, the circumstance to which you have alluded with so much humour is in proof of my assertion; and, to heighten my mortification at that time, my own family joined the popular cry, so that, in pronouncing all possibility of amendment,[6] the devoted prodigal was driven to a situation which absolutely precluded him from it.

"My father, in a long detail of my unworthiness, which, with his usual tenderness, he dealt forth to Harry de Salis, as a climax to the amiable history, concluded the list of my enormities with declaring that I actually intrigued with three different women of fashion at one and the same time! Without making any comment on the very creditable account given of me, and the favourable picture which his pious lordship displayed of our first-rate females, permit me to assure you that neither my prowess with the ladies, nor any foolish, unworthy deed of mine, occasioned the paternal displeasure of that moment. The subject of an occasional morning's reading was the true, but unacknowledged, cause of my disgrace. I shall do myself the justice of relating the fact to you in all its circumstances.

"You must have heard of the celebrated sceptical writer, Claude Anet. His works, and the prosecution which they brought upon him, have conspired to give his name no small share of public notoriety. It will be also necessary to inform you that, after the sacred writings, Lord Lyttelton has directed his partial estimation to two popular theological productions. The one details, explains, and observes upon the resurrection of Christ and the other defends the character and conduct of the Apostle Paul. The former was written by his dearly beloved friend, Mr. West; the latter by *himself.* The infidel, Claude Anet, among other matters, thought proper to give these two publications a particular and separate consideration. He had the abominable impudence to declare, that they were not only deficient in their principles, but that they were logically defective in the means they took to support them; nay, he undertakes to give them arguments superior to any they have used, and then to confute them.

"On this ground he opens his battery, and makes his attack; nor is he without his partisans among men of learning and talents, as I have been informed, who do not hesitate to assign him the victory. Of this I do not pretend to determine; I have, in truth, no genius for that line of criticism. The mode of proceeding, however, must be acknowledged to have been accompanied with an air of insolence and contempt which might have been the cause of mortification to men of a less sensible fibre than one, at least, of those against whom it was directed. It had this effect in the extreme for the pity of the Christian gave way to the pride of the author, and the damnable sceptic, instead of being the object of fervent prayer that he might be converted from the error of his way, was wafted, in a moment, by his pious antagonist, to the howling portion of the devil and his angels.

"In an unlucky hour it was discovered that this offensive volume was in my possession, and the subject of my occasional meditation; and from hence arose that unexpected burst of displeasure that fell with so much weight upon me, and which had instant recourse to my graceless life as the pretended reason for its justification. I do not know a quality of the human mind that is of such an absorbent nature as vanity; in one disappointed moment it will suck up the virtue of years. If Claude Anet had levelled his shafts in another direction, or I had increased my caution in tracing their course, I might have intrigued with a whole seraglio of women of fashion, without drawing upon me an atom of that vengeance of which I was the victim. I could not tell the true cause, as it would have increased, if possible, the irritation against me, without doing any good; and, besides, my authority would have been lighter than a feather, in the public opinion, when put in competition with the power that persecuted me for, religious opinions apart, the whole was an abominable persecution.

"I never felt so sensibly the inconvenience of a bad character as at this period. Impudence could do but little; hypocrisy, which is so thick a garb for half mankind, was not a veil of gauze to me; and, as for repentance, that was not in the reach of ordinary credibility. I was really in the situation of the Quaker's dog, who, being caught in the fact of robbing the pantry, was told, in all the complacency of revenge, by his amiable master, 'I will not beat thee, nor kill thee for thy thieving; but I will do worse, for I will give thee a bad name;' and immediately, on driving him from the house, alarmed the neighbourhood with the calm assurance that he was a mad dog; so that the poor animal was pursued with the unreflecting brutality usual on such occasions, which soon put an end to his existence. You may truly apply this story to your affectionate friend,

"[THOMAS LYTTELTON]."

He offended his uncle, Bishop Lyttelton, in a similar manner, according to the version of his disgrace with that prelate which he gives in a letter to a friend, of which the following is the greater and concluding portion:—

"Some years ago I had formed an unlucky plan to mortify my right reverend uncle, who had taken some authoritative liberties with me, without giving him a fair opportunity to express his resentment. This was no less than an attack upon the temporal privilege of episcopacy, in possessing a seat in the House of Lords. I had some thoughts of my own upon the subject, but I had fortunately added to their number and importance from the accidental perusal of a republished tract on the conduct of our bishops through upwards of twenty reigns, which unanswerably proved that, during so long a period, they had almost uniformly manifested themselves to be foes to rational liberty. I took up the argument in a very general view, urged it with modesty, and, what was better, with security, as, in case it had been returned with anger, I was armed with the opinion of my father, who was present, and, in his *Persian Letters*, has written to the same purpose. In short, I enjoyed all the triumph that my malicious expectation could have framed. The prelate grinned with vexation, but was forced to acquiesce in silence; and I had my revenge.

"But, not many days after, when my resentment towards this reverend relation had been lost in its fruition, a trifling circumstance happened, which his vigilant anger gladly seized, in order to heap upon me every indignity which his truly Christian spirit was capable of producing. As a family party of us were crossing the road on the side of Hagley Park, a chaise passed along, followed by a couple of attendants with French horns. 'Who can that be?' said my father. 'Some itinerant mountebank,' replied I, 'if one may judge from his musical followers.' I really spoke with all the indifference of an innocent mind; nor did it occur to me that the Right Reverend Father in God, my uncle, had sometimes been pleased to travel with servants accoutred with similar instruments.

But evil on itself will soon recoil,

and my recollection was soon restored to me by a torrent of abuse, which was, in length, violence, and, I had almost said, in expression, equal to any sacred anathema of popish resentment. In short, I was cursed, damned, and sent to the devil, in all the chaste periphrasis of a priest's implacability. The whole of the business was of a very singular nature: he availed himself of an inoffensive occurrence to let loose his resentment at a past offence; while I, in a state of actual innocence, sunk beneath the consciousness of past guilt.

"But, to conclude with a serious observation, be assured, my friend, that, however rich, great, or powerful a man may be, it is the height of folly to make personal enemies of any, but particularly from personal motives; for one unguarded moment—and who could support the horrors of a never-ceasing, suspicious vigilance!—may yield you to the revenge of the most despicable of mankind. From a very unpleasant experience of my own, I should most sincerely counsel every young man who is entering on the theatre of the world to merit the good opinion of mankind by an easy, unaffected, and amiable deportment to all, which will do more to make his walk through life respectable and happy, than those more striking and splendid qualities which are for ever in the extremes of honour or disgrace. Adieu!"

There is a strong resemblance between the position of Thomas Lyttelton at this period, and that of Mirabeau ten years later. Mirabeau, in 1781, plunged in profligacy and in debt, had returned to France after self-expatriation forced upon him by his misconduct, corrected and repentant, willing to amend, and longing to be reconciled to his family. But he knew not what to do with himself, nor did his father know what to do with him. The old marquis appealed to his brother, the Commander of the Order of Malta. "Have pity," he wrote, "on thy hurricane-nephew; he acknowledges, and with good reason, that the intellect and talent he employed in committing his follies are surprising; he admits this, like all the rest, for he is the greatest confessor of faults in the universe. It is impossible to possess greater intelligence and facility. With every attribute, or nearly so, of the sky-rocket, he is a thunder-bolt of labour and expedition. Example, knowledge, and superiority correct him of themselves; but he has an immense want of being governed. He knows that he owes his return to you; he knows that you have always been pilot and compass to me, and that you must be the same to him; and he puts his vanity in his uncle. I tell you he is a rare subject for the future. You have all the Saturn necessary for his Mercury. But if once you hold him, do not let him go; should he even perform miracles, keep your hold of him, and pull him by the sleeve, for the poor devil requires it."

"I will not have him," replied Commander Mirabeau. "If, at thirty-two years of age, he requires to be ridden with a curb rein, his understanding will never ripen. ... If, at his age, he is not sufficiently master of himself to avoid running his head against a post, it is madness to attempt to make anything of him."[7] Ten years after this correspondence, the name of Mirabeau was a potent spell to conjure with in the politics of his country. Thomas Lyttelton was four years younger, when he returned to his native country under similar circumstances, than the great Frenchman was when this correspondence passed between his father and his uncle. If Mirabeau's future was not to be despaired of at thirty-two, still less was Lyttelton's at twenty-eight.

1. "Letters of the late Lord Lyttelton." 1806.

2. "Correspondence of the Earl of Chatham." 1838.

3. "With great abilities, generally very ill applied—with a strong sense of religion, which he never suffered to influence his conduct—his days were mostly passed in splendid misery, and in the painful change of the most extravagant gaiety and the deepest despair. The delight, when he pleased, of the first and most select society, he chose to pass his time, for the most part, with the most profligate and abandoned of both sexes. Solitude was to him the most insupportable of all torments, and to banish reflection he flew to company whom he despised and ridiculed. This conduct was a source of bitter regret both to his father and to all his friends."—*Memoirs of Elizabeth Carter.*

4. "Memoirs and Letters of George Lord Lyttelton." 1845.

5. The author of the character of Thomas Lyttelton, prefixed to the volume of poems attributed to him, and published after his death. This brief essay is anonymous, but Roberts, who edited the volume, and wrote the preface, states that it was written by a gentleman who had been intimate with him.

6. There seems a slip of the pen here, unless we suppose a typographical blunder to have been made; the writer must have intended to say, "all amendment impossible."

7. "Memoirs of Mirabeau." 1842.

V

IMMORALITY AND MARRIAGE

THE MOST SUPERFICIAL reader that ever skimmed the cream of Horace Walpole's letters must rise from the perusal of that interesting mass of correspondence with the impression that the Georgian era was a most immoral one. Moral debasement and political corruption seemed to vie with each other for an odious and disgusting supremacy. Court and Cabinets, Lords and Commons, were all alike tainted with corruption and immorality. Those who were pointed out as vicious men were merely worse than the others; and it was one of the greatest misfortunes of the age that its affairs had to be conducted, as a rule, by bad men, because an Administration of the virtuous was rendered impracticable by the too frequent conjunction of mental dulness with moral purity.

Gambling and gallantry were vices from which few public men were free. The social pictures painted by Hogarth had not ceased to be truthful representations of a considerable section of English life and manners, though a little—perhaps a very little—abatement may have to be made from their grossness. The passion for cards and dice, and for betting, had received an enormous development. Lyttelton and the Damers, the Foxes and the Foleys, did not perhaps seek the perilous excitement of cards and dice in such dens as Hogarth painted, where there was no ballot for the admission of gamblers with pedigrees, to the exclusion of gamblers without, and where George Barrington and

Jack Rann could make a wager or throw the ivory cubes, without fear of interruption by Bow Street "runners," or those guardians of virtue, the parish constables. But high play went on nightly at all the clubs, and the best minds and hearts of the age were drawn into the fatal vortex. Fox, the school-fellow of Lyttelton and the Damers at Eton, and one day to be Prime Minister of England, equalled them in his rage for play, and exceeded them in the amount of his losses. Before he had attained his twenty-fourth year, his debts to Jew money-lenders amounted to the almost incredible sum of £100,000! He never won a large stake but once, when he gathered up £8,000 in crisp notes and bright guineas. But no loss ever ruffled his equanimity. Topham Beauclerk, a good-natured *roué* and ill-natured wit, calling upon him one morning, after a night of terrible losses at the card-table, found him calmly reading Herodotus. "What would you have me do," said Fox, on his visitor expressing surprise at the manner in which he bore his losses, "when I have lost my last shilling?"

Lord Coleraine and his two brothers squandered their patrimony at the gaming-table, and then cajoled or swindled their mother out of the £1,600 a year, which was all their demands upon his purse had allowed their father to bequeath to her, leaving her helpless and destitute, so that she became dependent upon a friend even for a bare subsistence. Then, as we learn from Horace Walpole, they sent for the poor lady, saying that her presence was necessary to some affair of business. "It was to show her to the Jews," says Walpole, "and convince them that hers was a good life, unless she is starved. You must not suppose that such actions are disapproved; for the second brother is going minister to Brussels, that he may not go to jail, whither he ought to go."

Betting ruinously supplemented the chances of cards and dice. The betting-books of White's and Brookes's contain bets on every conceivable subject—on the length of a life, the duration of a ministry, the result of an election, the sex of an unborn child, a convict's risk of the halter, or the truth about the latest scandal. Lord Nugent made a bet with Earl Temple that he would spit in the Earl of Bristol's hat; and the nasty wager was as nastily won, though it was very nearly resulting in a duel.[1] Lord Mountford bet Sir John Bland twenty guineas that Beau Nash would survive Colley Cibber. The same nobleman, when asked, soon after his daughter's marriage, whether she was in a condition to add to the number of his Majesty's subjects, replied, "Upon my word, I don't know; I have no bet upon it." Walpole says of him, that he "would have betted any man in England against himself for self-murder," so dominant was the passion for reducing everything to a calculation of chances. "There is a man about town," writes Walpole in 1768, "a Sir William Burdett, a man of very good family, but most infamous character. In short, to give you his character at once, there is a wager entered in the bet-book at White's, that the first baronet that will be hanged is this Sir William Burdett."

One day, a man fell down insensible before White's, and was carried into the house, where odds were immediately offered and taken as to whether he was dead or in a swoon. It was proposed to bleed him; but those who had betted that he was dead protested against the use of the lancet as affecting the fairness of the bet! Walpole tells a story of a clergyman, who, entering White's on the morning of the earthquake of 1750, and hearing bets laid whether the shock was caused by a natural convulsion of the earth, or by the explosion of a powder-mill, went away in horror, declaring that the members of the club were such an impious set that he believed, "if the last trump were to sound, they would bet puppet-show against judgment."

"You have won both your wagers," says Thomas Lyttelton, writing to a friend. "In speaking of the inhabitants of China, I *do* make use of the word *Chineses*; and I borrow the term from Milton. As to your first bet, that I used such an expression, your ears, I trust, will be grateful for the confidence you had in them. But your second wager, that, if I did use it, I had a good authority, is very flattering to myself; and I thank you for the opinion you entertain of the accuracy of my language. My memory will not, at this moment, direct you to the page, but you will readily find the word in the index of Newton's edition of Milton."

He made a singular bet with a gentleman name Blake, touching the virtue of a young woman named Harris, who was a waitress at an inn,[2] and whose beauty, wit, and coquetry had gained her many admirers, among whom were both the wagerers. Blake bet Lyttelton a hundred guineas that he would induce this girl to elope with him, and offered her all the money for her compliance. The offer was refused; and the girl's reputation for virtue seems to have been so high, that the refusal excited less surprise than her subsequent elopement with Lyttelton, who was probably aware of her preference for himself, and, therefore, the least surprised of the circle in which she was known. It is Sarah Harris who is referred to, under the name of Pomona, in the following letter:—

"[Ayscough] by no means deserves your pity; and the conduct which I have of late used, and shall continue to use, towards him, arises from my perfect knowledge of his character, and the remembrance of his former treatment of myself. I told you long ago, when my bulrush hung its head, that, high as this gentleman then bore himself, the time would come when he would hang his head in his turn, and bend his back for me to tread upon. All this and more is now come to pass.

"You express your surprise that he does not discover some degree of resentment on the occasion of his last journey to Hagley. The fever of that business flushed him with no small hope, and the succeeding ague shook him with disappointment; but he had the prudence to conceal his symptoms, and I left him to cure himself. He may bluster in a guard-room with new commissioned ensigns, and, in the leisure of a tilt-yard duty, may weave fanciful wreaths of future fame; nay, he may venture to give his name to the world in a newspaper, or the title-page of a miserable poem; but the prowess of our hero will go farther.[3] If I were to bid him go to the Pomona of Hocknel for a pippin, he would not hesitate a moment, and would burn his fingers willingly in roasting it; and, when I had eaten the pulp, he would content himself with the core.

> All this my little Greek exactly knows,
> And bid him go to hell, to hell he goes.

"If, however, your obstinate humanity should look towards such an object, have a little patience, and he will give you an opportunity for the full exercise of it. I am in the secret, but I shall not gratify his vanity by betraying it. After all, I find him convenient, and to my purpose. He is ready, submissive, and not without amusement. If he were to die, I should say with Shakespeare, *'I could have better spared a better man.'*

"At this moment, he is sitting on the other side of my table, in the act of making some of his own bad poetry worse, in which agreeable business I may, perhaps, be kind enough to give him some assistance. You would not, probably, have suspected him in so close a vicinity to me, but it is a fact; and when I have folded up my letter, he shall enclose it in its envelope, and set the seal to this certificate of his own good qualities; nay, I will make him direct it into the bargain. Your pence, it is true, will suffer for this whim of mine, but the revenue will be a gainer—a circumstance which must satisfy you as a patriot, on the truly political idea of making follies productive to the State. You may observe, however, and with some reason, that every one should pay for his own. To such a remark I have nothing to answer, but that I am," &c.

His amour with Sarah Harris was made the subject of a ribald and indecent poem, entitled "The Rape of Pomona," which the compiler of the catalogue of the library of the British Museum attributes to him, though it is stated, in the preface, to be the production of a Cambridge student, whose passion for the beautiful waitress had induced him to locate himself under the same roof with her, in the humble capacity of a waiter. However this may be, the poem is written in the assumed character of Bolton's waiter, and edited by John Courtney, a gentleman who then represented the little borough of Tamworth in Parliament, and was probably a worthy associate of the Damers, the Foleys, the Foxes, and other tavern-haunting, dice-throwing nominees of the owners of rotten boroughs. If Courtney was not himself the author of the doggerel, it may have been written by Combe, who, having dissipated his fortune by gambling, was, in 1771, found by a friend at an inn at Swansea, in the position of waiter. Combe, however, completed his education at Oxford, not at Cambridge. There is an allusion in the poem to a lady named Dawson, who is described in a note as "a foolish widow who chose to make Mr. L—tt—n the guardian of her person and fortune, and enjoys the fruits of her credulity." It is incredible that this would have been written by Lyttelton himself; even if he could be proved to have been capable of writing, and giving to the world, such a ribald and obscene composition. The extract is given here because it fixes the date of an amour to which public attention was subsequently called by Sir Nathaniel Wraxall,[4] in his usual blundering manner, as will hereafter be shown.

The following letter, on the comparative influence of reason and the passions, may most appropriately be introduced in this place:—

"MY DEAR FRIEND,—Your letter, which I received no longer ago than yesterday, would do honour to the most celebrated name among the moral writers of any period. It is the most sensible, easy, and concise history of the passions I have ever read. Indeed, it has never been my lot to have given any great portion of my time to such studies. These powers have kept me too much in the sphere of their own tumultuous whirlwinds to leave me the leisure of examining them. I have been, am, and I fear shall be, their sport and their slave; and when I shall acquire that serenity of character which will enable me to examine them with a philosophical scrutiny, I cannot tell. My expectations are at such a distance on this point, that I am almost ashamed to mention my apprehensions to you. It is, however, treating you with the confidence you deserve, to tell you that from my soul I think the very source of them must be dried up before they will lose their empire over me. In the lively expression of the poet, 'they are the elements of life,' without which man would be a mass of insensible and unintelligent matter. Now, it is that happy compound of these elementary particles of intellectual life that you so well describe, so thoroughly understand, and so happily possess, which I despair of attaining. I have the resolution to make resolutions, but it extends no farther—I cannot keep them; and to escape from the misery brought on by one passion, I have so habituated myself to bathe in a branch of the same flood, that I cannot look for any other relief.

"You very naturally ask me where all this must end? I know not!—and to similar interrogatories I have sometimes madly replied, I care not! But I shall not offend you with such a declaration; and when I am writing to you, I do not feel disposed to do it. In answering you, therefore, I shall adopt the language of the ruined gamester, who addressed his shadow in the glass:—'*Je vous ai dit et reclit, Malheureux! que si vous continuez à faire de pareil tours, vous iriez à l'hôpital.*'

"You lay great stress upon the powers of reason, and, in truly philosophical language, heightened by the most proper and affecting imagery, present this sage directress of weak mortals to my attention. I receive her at your hand; respect her as your friend; and venerate her as the cause of your superiority over me; but whether she perceives that my respect is insincere, or remembers how shamefully I have neglected her, so it is that she slides insensibly from me, and I see her no more. My bark rides steady for a moment, but it is not long ere it again becomes the sport of winds and billows. But after all, and without any blasphemous arraignment of the order of Providence, permit me to ask you, why is this principle—implanted in our natures for the wise and happy regulation of them—so weak in itself, so slow in its progress, and so late in its maturity? If it is designed to control our passions, why does it not keep pace with them? Wherefore does it not *grow with their growth, and strengthen with their strength?* And what cause can be assigned that the one are ripe for gratification before the other has scarce bursted into blossom?

"Let us, however, take a long stride from the imbecility of youth to the firmness of mature age, and we shall see that the passions have only changed their form; that reason still totters, is frequently driven from her throne, and even deserts those who have most cultivated her friendship and acknowledged her power. The contest frequently continues through life, and the superiority as often ends, where it always begins—on the side of passion. We may be said even sometimes to outlive reason; while passion of some kind, and many times of the worst kind, will preserve its influence to the last. To conclude the matter, how often does the lamp of human reason become extinct, yielding corporal nature a prey to passion in the extreme, whose tortures are rendered more fierce by the iron restraints of necessary policy and medical interposition!

"If it were possible to trace the course of reason in the mind of the best man that ever lived, from its first budding to a fulness of maturity, what a mortifying scene would be unveiled! What checks and delays, what tranquillity and tumult, what frequent extinction and renovation, what rapid flights and sudden downfalls, what contest and submission, would compose the operations of this rightful mistress of human actions? Men of cold tempers, and habituated to reflection, may cry up this distinctive faculty of man; they may chaunt its apotheosis, and build temples to its honour: such were Lord Shaftesbury and Mr. Addison; and they may be joined by those whose fortunate education and early connections have given to their warmer dispositions the best objects; in that confined but happy society I must place my friend, whose kind star preserved his youth from temptation, and blest his bloom of manhood with the ample and all-satisfying pleasures of virtuous love. You will not suspect me of wishing to diminish the reality of that merit which I so much admire, or of a desire to damp the glow of that virtue whose lustre cannot be diminished by my envy, or heightened by my praise; but, in the course of human affairs, time and chance have so much to do, that I cannot suppose even your worth to be without some obligations to them.

"To conclude this very, very long letter, I must beg leave to observe that I do not understand why reason, that divinity of philosophers, should be cooped up in the confined region of

the brain, while the passions are permitted to range at large, and
without restraint, through every other part of the body. I see
you smile; but be assured that these two jarring powers are, for a
moment, both united in me, to assure you that I am, with a real
sincerity, yours, &c"

There was living at this time, at the Leasowes, that rural paradise
of Shenstone, a lady named Peach, to whom had been given at her
baptism the unique name of Apphia. She was the second daughter
of Broome Witts, a gentleman residing at Chipping Norton; and
the widow of Joseph Peach, late Governor of Calcutta. Still young,
and according to contemporary accounts, as amiable as she was
beautiful, she attracted the attention of Thomas Lyttelton, and
seems to have encouraged it under the delusion fostered by the
old adage—"A reformed rake makes the best husband." It may be
gathered from the following letter, that, on his part, the preference
amounted to no more than the absence of dislike; and that he was
impelled to the thought of marriage by the insufficiency of the
allowance he received from his father:—

"Have you ever by chance looked into a book on the science of
cookery? If so, have you not observed that the culinary disciple
is instructed, when certain quantities of gravy, or essence, or
conserves, are prepared, to put them by for use? Now, if we
could manage our ideas in the same manner—if we could lock
up our acquired thoughts and knowledge in a kind of intellectual
store-room, from whence they might be drawn forth for
application—we should no longer be the slaves of a capricious
recollection, which at this hour offers its treasures with intuitive
readiness, yields them on the morrow with sullen reluctance, and
on the succeeding day may refuse them to our most arduous
researches. The active events of life, however, seldom die on the
remembrance: and you must certainly be mistaken in associating
with me the circumstance you mention in your letter, which is
at this instant before me. It is morally impossible that I should
have forgotten it. My memory, perhaps, is the only faculty I

possess which has not at one time or other deceived me; nay, so firm is its texture, that the oblivious hours of courtship do not affect its wonted capacities—though, to say the truth, mine is a very drowsy progress. Assiduity without love, tenderness without sincerity, and dalliance without desire, afford the miserable, the hopeless, but the faithful picture of my sluggish journey to the temple of Hymen. However, to give something of colour to the intervening hours between consent and fruition, his lordship performs wonders, and sighs and flatters for his heedless son; nay, he tunes his lyre, and sings the power of those charms which, by an anti-Circean fascination, are destined, by his fancy, to recall my vagrant footsteps to the paths of virtue. But, alas! I know not the resolution of the Greeks; I cannot resist the song of the syrens, and, partial as I may be to paternal music, it will prove, in its influence upon me, far inferior to theirs.

"But all is not torpor and inanimation, and what love could not produce, vanity has inspired. Two of the brethren of the house of my Dulcinea made her a visit last week, with the design of turning her from the expectation of a coronet, and from me. I need not tell you that they are honest, simple *bourgeois*, or they would not have meditated such a fruitless errand to their ambitious sister. I was well assured that they would not convert her; and the fancy came across me to aim at converting them. In this business I so exerted myself in every form of attention, flattery, and amusement, that I verily believe they returned to their home at Chipping Norton, without enforcing that remonstrance which was the object of their journey.

"That Chipping Norton—in whose neighbourhood I passed with my grandmother many of my youthful days, and to which I had never associated any idea but that of pigs playing upon organs—that chilly Chipping Norton should yield one of its former toasts to be the *cara sposa* of your friend! What can your fertile fancy deduce from the union of Hagley's genius and the widowed protectress of the more than widowed Leasowes? If offspring there should be, what a strange demitheocrite will owe its being to such a Hymen! Alas! my friend, this is but a dream for your amusement; the reality will offer to your compassionate experience the marriage of infatuation and necessity, whose legitimate and certain issue will be a separate maintenance, and perhaps a titled dowry.

"I have many and various communications to make to you, but they must be reserved for personal intercourse. In the meantime, when you shall see me announced as being added to the Benedicks of the year, save me, I beseech you, save me your congratulations. Nothing is so absurd as the tide of felicitations. which flow in upon a poor newly-married man, before he himself can determine—and much less the complimenting world—upon the propriety of them. Marriage is the grand lottery of life; and it is as great a folly to exult upon entering into it, as on the purchase of a ticket in the State wheel of fortune. It is when the ticket is drawn a prize that we can answer to congratulations. Adieu!"

There is no act of Thomas Lyttelton's life that presents so many difficulties to the biographer as his marriage. The contrast between the tone of the foregoing letter and that of the more brief epistles which he addressed to his father just before his union, and on his wedding-day—the contradiction to the suspicion of hypocrisy which is afforded by the openness and candour displayed in his acts, and in the expression of his thoughts and feelings on every other occasion—the suddenness with which the event was broought about, during his visit to the Leasowes—the agreement of the result with the dark vaticinations of the letter just given, constitute a problem in the science of the human heart which will probably never be solved.

It is certain, however, that Lord Lyttelton represented the match to his friends as the result of an ardent and reciprocal attachment, from which everything was to be hoped; and that similar representations were made to him both by his son and by Mrs. Peach. Some light might perhaps be thrown upon the matter if we knew the duration of Thomas Lyttelton's stay at the Leasowes before the marriage took place; what took place between the parties and the brothers of Mrs. Peach; and what caused the marriage to take place suddenly, and without the knowledge of Lord Lyttelton. But upon these points we are in the dark, and the family archives at Hagley Hall have unfolded for me only the following contributions to their elucidation:—

"My Dear Lord,—It is unnecessary for me to tell you I am as happy as it is possible for me to be: if anything could add to my present felicity, it would be your lordship's company. Lord Temple's letter was equally agreeable to Mrs. Peach and myself. I own I ever was proud of his presentiment in my favour. My dearest little woman is everything to me—the sweetest companion, the most sensible friend, and will make the best of wives. She unites almost contradictory excellencies. Adieu, my dear lord. I remain, ever your most dutiful and most obliged son,

"T.H. Lyttelton.
"Leasowes, *June* 18*th*, 1772."

At the back of this, Mrs. Peach wrote as follows:—

"Mr. Lyttelton persuades me that your lordship will receive, as a mark of my entire respect, this hasty and irregular assurance of the tender and unutterable affection that my improved acquaintance with the amiableness of his manners and the ten thousand dormant virtues of his heart have excited in my mind. It will be the delightful employment of my life to preserve his love and enlarge his happiness—fortunate beyond expression should I succeed—since it may secure to me the additional blessing of your lordship's approbation, and draw a veil over the many weaknesses and imperfections that the candour of your noble family does not allow them to attribute to, my lord, your lordship's most faithful and most obliged servant,

"Apphia Peach."

Eight days afterwards, on the 26th of June, 1772, they were married in the parish church of Hales Owen, the bridegroom betraying an absence of mind on the occasion, which must have been as mortifying to the bride as it was ominous of the future. The story is told by Lyttelton himself as follows:—

"If I am not very much mistaken, your library table is always furnished with an inter-leaved Bruyère, on whose blank pages you amuse yourself with extending the ideas of that celebrated writer, or directing them to modern applications. I am, therefore, to offer my name as an addition to your collections, and to desire that in your *scholia* on that excellent work, I may furnish a trait to his admirable character of the absent man.

"On the day of my marriage, a day—but no more of that! After the nuptial benediction was over, and we were returning to our equipage, instead of being the gallant Benedick, and conducting the new-made Mrs. [Lyttelton] to her coach, I slouched on before, and was actually getting into the carriage, as if I had been quite alone; but, recollecting myself as my foot was upon the step, I turned round to make my apology, which completed the business, for I addressed the bride in her widowed name, with 'My dear Mrs. [Peach], I beg ten thousand pardons,' and so on. This fit of absence was as strange as it proved ridiculous—an omen, perhaps, of all the ungracious business which is to follow. You may first laugh at this little foolish history, and then, if you please, apply it to a more serious purpose.

"But this species of absence is an hereditary virtue. A virtue! say you? Yes, sir, a virtue; for it is a mark of genius, and my right honourable father possesses it in a most flattering degree. I will present you with a most remarkable example, which you may also add to the composition of your modern Theophrastus. His lordship was about to pay a morning sacrifice at the shrine of M——, and a large bunch of early pinks lay upon his toilette, which were to compose the offering of the day. With those antique or professional beaux who wear the tie or large flowing wig, it appears to be convenient, in the ceremony of their dress, that the head should bring up the rear, and be covered the last. The full-trimmed suit was put on, the sword was girded to his side, the *chapeau de bras* was compressed by his left arm, the bunch of pinks graced his right hand, and his night-cap remained upon his pate. The servant having left the room, the venerable peer, forgetful of his perukean honours, would actually have sallied forth into the street in full array, and *en bonnet de nuit* if his *valet de chambre* had not arrived, at the critical moment to prevent his singular exit. I was present, but my astonishment at his figure so totally suspended my faculties, that he would have made the length of Curzon Street before I should have recovered any power of reflection. I was accused, as you may suspect, of a purposed inattention, in order to render his lordship ridiculous; and, I was told upon the occasion, that, although this kind of occasional absence of mind might furnish folly with laughter, it generally arose from that habitual exertion of thought which produces wisdom. You may congratulate me, therefore, on the prospect of my advancement to the title of sage.

"I am already married, and what is to follow, God alone knows. Strange things daily happen *dans ce bas monde*, and things more strange may be behind. I have such a budget to open for you but that discovery must be reserved till we meet. Suffice it to say at present—

> *Quædam parva quidem, sed non toleranda maritis."*

This unrestrained communication of the feelings with which the writer entered upon married life evinces a state of things most unpromising for the domestic felicity of the young couple. What could be hoped for from an union of which one of the parties had, before marriage, predicted that the result would be a separation? The event was announced to Lord Lyttelton by his son on the same day, in the following letter:—

"Leasowes, *26th June*, 1772.
"MY DEAR LORD,—I was this day so fortunate as to lead Mrs. Peach to the altar. I need not tell your lordship that the impatience and ardour of a lover was one chief cause that determined my fair bride; your Lordship's letter was another motive that operated on

her gentle mind. She is a woman of exceeding generosity of spirit and principle. Nothing, my dear lord, is wanting to perfect my felicity but your company; nothing else is wanted to complete her happiness. I wait with eagerness for the moment when I shall have the honour of presenting Mrs. Lyttelton to her father. Adieu, my dear lord. In all states and circumstances of my life, believe me to be, with unfeigned affection, your lordship's most dutiful son, and most obliged servant,

"T. Lyttelton.

"I shall again write to your lordship by to-morrow's post."

The promise conveyed in the postscript was redeemed in the following letter:—

"Leasowes, 27th June, 1772.

"My Dear Lord,—I promised your lordship yesterday to write to you by this day's post, as I thought you would be desirous of knowing what articles had been drawn, and what promises I had entered into. The only article settled by me previous to my marriage was the settlement of a jointure on my wife in case she survived me, so far as I was enabled to settle it, which is only from the time of your lordship's decease. This settlement is £1,000 a year, which is all that is in my power to appoint.

"I remain, therefore, exactly in the same situation as before my marriage took place, with the addition of her fortune. Concerning the disposition of it, I have entered into no agreement, but have (previous to my marriage) explained to my wife, and to the gentleman who married us, and who is an intimate friend of hers, what were my intentions. They both approved of them, and it is my desire to carry those intentions into execution as soon as possible; but my respect and duty to your lordship make me wish to lay the plan before you, and I hope it will in all particulars meet with your approbation, and that, though I am free to act as I think proper, you will find that I mean to do everything consistent both with my honour and interest, which terms, if well understood, are synonymous.

"I wait, therefore, with impatience, for your lordship's arrival to ratify and confirm my happiness, and I flatter myself I shall every day make myself more worthy of your regard and affection. Adieu, my dear father. Believe me ever your most dutiful son and obliged and obedient servant,

"T. LYTTELTON."

"Mrs. Lyttelton desires her dutiful respects to your lordship."

The Earl of Chatham conveyed his congratulations on the event to Lord Lyttelton in the following terms:—

"MY DEAR LORD,—I have a most longing wish to be able to be the bearer of my warm felicitations to your lordship and the happy pair on the completion of an union which knits you all together for life in the sweet triple bonds of paternal, filial, conjugal love and domestick happiness; may the virtues of your race guard the pious work, and fix the felicity of your family on that *fortuna domûs et avi numerentur avorum!* I could not but smile to hear that Cupid knew his Hagley for true Paphian ground, and had taught his slow brother Hymen to mend his pace in so delightful a race, and am sure your lordship has more than forgiven your flesh and blood this amiable impatience. From all I hear of Mrs. Lyttelton, I have not the least doubt that Hymen now will have his turn, and lead Love for his inseparable companion. Lady Chatham desires to be included in the same cordial sentiments with myself on whatever interests your lordship's happiness, and that of your family."

Lord Lyttelton says in his reply, after thanking his noble correspondent for his felicitations:—

"My son stole a march upon me, which I shall not complain of if he continues as sensible of the prize he was in such haste to take as he was when he took it; and I do not despair that he will. For my own part the more I see of the lady the more I esteem and love her. They both desire me to present their most respectful compliments and thanks to your lordship and Lady Chatham, and to all their amiable young friends at Burton Pynsent."

What a contrast between these letters and those of the bridegroom! The congratulations of Lord Chatham seem like the sunshine that gilds the waves, after a storm in which some noble vessel has been submerged, while the dusky sea-plants wave beneath above the corpses of the drowned mariners. While the two peers are exchanging compliments, we seem to hear, through the hum of friendly felicitations and a haze of orange blossoms and white lace, the ominous words,—"assiduity without love, tenderness without sincerity, dalliance without desire!"

1. Sir Nathaniel Wraxall's "Memoirs of my own Times," vol. i.
2. "Bolton's inn at Hockrel."—Preface to *The Rape of Pomona*. Thomas Lyttelton, in a letter presently to be quoted, calls the place Hocknel. It is not to be found by either name in any gazetteer.
3. It seems probable that the word "no" has been inadvertently omitted before "farther," either by the writer or the printer.
4. "Memoirs of My Own Time." 1836.